P9-DGF-764

THE
WAR
ON THE
POOR

A DEFENSE MANUAL

**RANDY ALBELDA, NANCY FOLBRE, AND
THE CENTER FOR POPULAR ECONOMICS**

The New Press, New York

© 1996 by Randy Albelda, Nancy Folbre, and the Center for Popular Economics

All rights reserved. No part of this book may be reproduced in any form without
written permission from the publisher.

Library of Congress Catalog Card Number 96-67176
ISBN 1-56584-262-6

Published in the United States by The New Press, New York
Distributed by W. W. Norton & Company, Inc., New York

Established in 1990 as a major alternative to the large, commercial publishing
houses, The New Press is a full-scale nonprofit American book publisher outside
of the university presses. The Press is operated editorially in the public interest,
rather than for private gain; it is committed to publishing in innovative ways
works of educational, cultural, and community value that, despite their intellec-
tual merits, might not normally be commercially viable. The New Press's editorial
offices are located at the City University of New York.

Book design by Knickerbocker and Leah Lococo

Printed in the United States of America

9 8 7 6 5 4 3

Peter Kuper

KUPER

TABLE OF CONTENTS

TABLE OF CONTENTS

Maria Olsen / Impact Visuals

ACKNOWLEDGMENTS

This book was truly a collaborative effort. We called on both new and long-time friends, colleagues, and collaborators for their help. This book would still be only an idea without their design, writing, research, and financial contributions. We thank them for their generosity and their talents.

Research Coordinator

Lois Yachetta

Research and Editing

Elissa Braunstein

Lynn Duggan

Robert Dworak

James Heintz

Tiffany Manuel

Patricia Murray

Ann Robbart

Val Voorheis

Kristin White

Lois Yachetta

Design

Knickerbocker

Leah Lococo

Contributors

Barbara Bergmann

Cyann Brolfe

Deborah M. Figart

Linda Gordon

Heidi Hartmann

June Lapidus

Frances Fox Piven

Theda Skocpol

William J. Wilson

Comments and Suggestions

Martha Ackelsberg

Teresa Amott

Lisa Bernstein

Carly Berwick

Françoise Carré

Lynn Duggan

Robert Dworak

Linda Gordon

James Heintz

Carol Heim

Cindy Mann

Arthur MacEwan

Michael Meeropol

Elaine McCrate

Frances Fox Piven

Betsy Reed

Ellen Reeves

William Reeves

Ann Robbart

Dawn Saunders

Lisa Saunders

Steve Savner

Robert Schaeffer

Carrie Schoen

Hall Smyth

Chris Tilly

Ann Withorn

Financial Support

The John D. and Catherine T. MacArthur Foundation

The Unitarian Universalist Veatch Program at Shelter Rock

John Maher Fund of the Funding Exchange

The James R. Dougherty Foundation

The Haymarket People's Fund

1995 was not a good year for poor people or for those who cared about them. Politicians from both parties proposed legislation to slash funding for welfare programs and mandated a new block grant system designed to eliminate entitlements to assistance. Many states imposed new punitive restrictions on recipients. Previous attacks on poor people's programs during the Reagan-Bush years seem like minor skirmishes compared with the Republican barrage masterminded by Speaker of the House Newt Gingrich.

The new political war on the poor features systematic efforts to discredit public assistance. Its generals denounce the War on Poverty as a total failure. Its chaplains preach that single mothers deserve the blame for most of society's problems. Its politicians declare that poor families would be happier and better off with less. Compliant journalists write feature stories about recipients who agree that dependency is bad without mentioning that abject poverty is even worse.

This campaign is well organized and well financed. But it is meeting with fierce resistance from a broad cross section of Americans who believe that a decent society must care for—and care about—all its members. No society that allows large numbers of children to grow up in poverty can pretend to offer equal opportunity to all its citizens. This defense manual was written to help people who believe in democratic ideals fight for our collective right to a generous and effective safety net. It was also designed to enlist broader public participation in debates over the future of the welfare state.

Our purpose is not to defend the major public assistance programs that remained in effect through 1995: Aid to Families with Dependent Children, Food Stamps, and Medicaid. We agree that these programs have serious shortcomings. However, many criticisms of them have been inaccurate and misleading, and most of the proposed alternatives would do even greater harm. As the congressional legislative agenda has unfolded, it has become increasingly clear that so-called reforms for the poor largely entail cutting costs for the rich.

The first part of this book directly confronts the most aggressive conservative myths, challenging them with fully documented facts and figures. Six chapters explore the myths and realities of issues ranging from "The Welfare State" to "Sex, Lies, and Righteous Indignation." Each topic is vividly illustrated in a modular format that allows for quick reading and easy excerpting. The second part provides more narrative background, combining a variety of factual presentations and brief articles. Chapter 7 provides an overview of poverty and public assistance policies that includes contributions by Linda Gordon and Frances Fox Piven. Chapter 8 prescribes a variety of ways that advocates for the poor can move beyond a purely defensive strategy, with short pieces by Theda Skocpol and William J. Wilson, Barbara Bergmann and Heidi Hartmann, Deborah Figart and June Lapidus, and Cyann Brolfe. Chapter 9 offers an annotated guide to federal social programs for low-income people that remained in effect in 1995, for readers who might otherwise be puzzled by acronyms such as AFDC (Aid to Families with Dependent Children) or EITC (Earned Income Tax Credit). Also included is a list of organizations, resource centers, and research materials designed to help activists keep up-to-date with economic and legislative trends.

Many pundits and politicians in this country are making careers out of demonizing poor people. Their claims are morally wrong and economically bankrupt and will provide only a temporary distraction from an underlying problem that politicians are reluctant to face. Over the last 20 years, economic growth has failed to improve earnings for all but the most highly educated workers. Slashing social spending for the disabled, elders, and mothers raising children on their own will not balance the budget. It will not strengthen the family. It will not punish the wicked. It will only make more people poor.

The
Welfare
State

Mel Rosenthal / Impact Visuals

MYTH

"My friends, some years ago, the federal government declared war on poverty, and poverty won."[1]
—Ronald Reagan, President

"The Liberal Welfare State has been a colossal failure."[2]
—Republican Study Committee

REALITY

The War on Poverty didn't fail. It was called off. Federal antipoverty programs put in place in 1964 steadily reduced the percentage of people living in poverty until the late 1970s, when many states began letting inflation erode the value of monthly payments to families with dependent children. In effect, state legislators called a truce, if not a full-scale retreat. Then, in 1980, President Reagan's inaugural speech rallied conservatives around a war on welfare that gradually gathered support from many elected Democrats as well as Republicans.

Poverty rates have increased since the 1970s partly because of cutbacks in public assistance. The average value of monthly payments provided by Aid to Families with Dependent Children (AFDC) has not kept pace with inflation, and modest increases in Food Stamps have not been sufficient to compensate. By July 1994, the real value of average Food Stamps and AFDC payments was 20% lower than it had been in July 1971.[4]

Higher unemployment rates and declining real wages for workers without college diplomas have also contributed to higher poverty rates.[5] If it weren't for public assistance, poverty rates would be much higher.

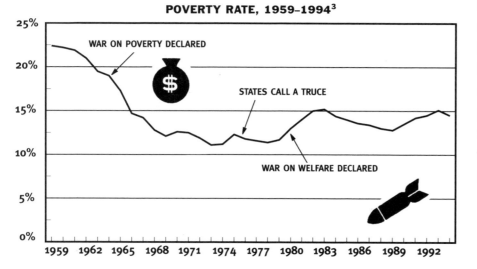

POVERTY RATE, 1959–1994[3]

WAR ON POVERTY DECLARED

STATES CALL A TRUCE

WAR ON WELFARE DECLARED

25% 20% 15% 10% 5% 0%

1959 1962 1965 1968 1971 1974 1977 1980 1983 1986 1989 1992

- In 1992, 15% of all Americans had incomes under the poverty line. In the absence of government income transfers (including AFDC, Social Security, and Supplemental Security Income), 24% would have had incomes under the poverty line.[6]

"Has every defense contractor yielded a perfect product, at minimal cost? Has every cancer project brought a cure? Has every space launching succeeded? Has every diplomatic initiative brought peace? Why should a less than perfect record for social programs be less tolerable to society than failed economic, military, or diplomatic policies?"[7]

HYMAN BOOKBINDER, poverty program administrator under President Lyndon Johnson

Paul Corio

MYTH "To the average man on the street, to say someone is poor implies that he is malnourished, poorly clothed, and lives in filthy, dilapidated, and overcrowded housing. In reality there is little material poverty in the U.S. in the sense generally understood by the public."[8]
—Heritage Foundation, conservative think tank

"I didn't agree to take a vow of poverty."[9]
—William Bennett, declining to take a job as national chairman of the Republican party at a salary of $125,000 per year

REALITY

Most people don't realize just how low the poverty line is.

- In 1995, the poverty line for a single person was $7,470; for a family of 3, $12,590; for a family of 4, $15,150.[10]

- When asked by a Gallup poll in 1989 what amount of income they would use as a poverty line for a family of 4 in their community, the average person's response was 24% higher than the official poverty line in that year.[11]

The official poverty line understates the number of people living in need. Government estimates of poor people's incomes do not include measures of the value of Food Stamps or Medicaid. If these are added, fewer people currently have incomes under the official

THE INVISIBLE POOR! BY ED SUBITZKY

OOPS! SORRY! CARL, IS THAT YOU?

NO, BOB! IT'S ME, ERNIE!

SURE IS ROUGH NOT BEING SEEN, ISN'T IT!

IT STARTED WHEN OUR FELLOW AMERICANS WOULDN'T RECOGNIZE US!

THEN CAME CONGRESS!

CARE TO HELP A FELLA, SIR? MY FOOD STAMPS RAN OUT TWO DAYS AGO!

I WAS VISIBLE UNTIL MY COMPANY DOWNSIZED!

YOU'D THINK MY KIDS WERE AWFUL CUTE AND DESERVING IF YOU COULD SEE THEM!

HE DIDN'T EVEN KNOW WE WERE HERE!

SAY, HOW MANY OF US ARE THERE, ANYWAY?

HOW COULD WE POSSIBLY KNOW?

SALLY, YOU AND I ALWAYS GET ALONG SO WELL...

poverty line. But this line is too low.

- It was defined by the federal government in the 1960s as the amount of money required for a subsistence diet multiplied by 3 because most families spent about a third of their income on food. Current spending patterns are very different: Families spend a smaller percentage on food because they must spend a larger percentage on housing and transportation. A poverty-level income is no longer sufficient to meet basic needs.[12]

- Family incomes have increased more rapidly than the poverty

Impact Visuals

line. As a result, poor people's incomes are much lower relative to other people's incomes than they used to be. In the early 1960s, the poverty line equaled about one-half of median income. It now equals about one-third.[13]

- The official poverty line ignores the costs of paid work for adults in families with children. A single mother (or father) who works outside the home must pay for child care; although she earns income, she also incurs more expenses. The poverty line should be higher for families without a full-time caretaker.[14]

- A panel of nonpartisan experts from the National Academy of Sciences has recommended increasing the poverty line and changing the way it is calculated.[15]

Ed Subitzky

MYTH

"In 1992, federal, state, and local governments spent $305 billion on means-tested welfare programs for low-income Americans. Welfare now absorbs 5% of the Gross National Product, up from 1.5% in 1965 when the War on Poverty began."[16]
—The Heritage Foundation

"Government has spent $5.3 trillion on welfare since the War on Poverty began—and we lost the war."[17]
—Rep. Bill Archer, R-Texas

REALITY

The Heritage Foundation estimate is misleading.

- It includes many expenditures that are not restricted to the poor, such as the Earned Income Tax Credit (EITC), and some that are not even restricted to low-income families, such as student loan and school lunch programs.

- It also includes the value of all spending on Medicaid, though more than half of this is spent on the blind, the disabled, and the elderly and does not benefit the group that most people think of as welfare recipients—families getting AFDC.

- Adding this number up for all years since 1965 generates a dramatic but meaningless figure.

A better estimate of welfare spending in 1992 is about $70.5 billion.

- Federal and state governments spent a total of $43 billion on two major means-tested programs for the poor, AFDC and Food Stamps. Medicaid expenditures on families receiving AFDC in that year amounted to $27.5 billion.[18]

- By this definition, welfare spending amounted to about 1.2% of Gross Domestic Product in 1992, and federal welfare spending amounted to about 5% of the federal budget.[19]

Increases in welfare spending since 1980 largely reflect the rapid escalation of all medical costs, which has increased Medicaid spending.

- Between 1980 and 1993, total spending on AFDC and Food Stamps declined as a percentage of Gross Domestic Product (GDP) from 0.8% to 0.7%. Over the same time period, federal spending on these programs has declined as a percentage of the federal budget from 3.2% to 2.4%.[20]

MYTH

"The standard AFDC wage and benefits package is between $13,000 and $20,000 per year."[21]
—Republican Study Committee

"Many Welfare Mamas are, as the old-timers used to say, very 'fleshy,' sucking on cigarettes, with booze and soft drinks in the fridge, feeding their faces with fudge as they watch the color TV."[22]
—Don Boys, former member of the Indiana House of Representatives

The standard package for a family of 3 receiving AFDC, Food Stamps, and Medicaid is worth about $11,000.

- The average value of benefits received by a family of 3 on AFDC and Food Stamps in 1992 was $7,362. The average spent on AFDC recipients through Medicaid in the same year was $1,221 per person, or $3,363 per family. The total comes to $10,725 per 3-person family, or $3,575 per person.[24]

Public assistance in the form of AFDC and Food Stamps is low and getting lower.

- In 1992, the average AFDC benefit per recipient was $136 per month. The average value of Food Stamp benefits per recipient was $68.50 per month.[25] In terms of purchasing power, these benefit levels are 20% lower than they were in 1970.[26]

REALITY

The Republican estimate is wrong.

- It incorrectly assumes that all AFDC recipients get housing subsidies, supplemental food from Women, Infants, and Children Food and Nutrition Services (WIC), free or reduced-price school meals, and Food Stamps. It also includes a high estimate of the value of health care provided by Medicaid.

- In 1992, 30% of AFDC recipients lived in public or subsidized rental housing, 22% received WIC benefits, and 86% received Food Stamps.[23]

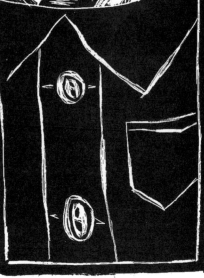

- Many poor people get no assistance at all. In 1992, only 43% of the poor collected cash assistance, and only slightly more than half benefited from Food Stamps or Medicaid.[27]

- In 1992, only 25% of all single-parent families were lifted out of poverty by government assistance, compared with 39% in 1979.[28]

"I'm not knocking the welfare program, because it's a lifesaver—it's there. Because you've got a roof over your head and you're not out in the street. But on the other hand, as far as my own situation is concerned, it's pretty rough living this way. I can't see anybody that would ever settle for something like this just for the mere fact of getting a free ride, because it's not worth it."[29]

51-YEAR-OLD DIVORCED MOTHER ON WELFARE

Melinda Beck

MYTH

"The poor in this country are the biggest piglets at the mother pig and her nipples. . . . They're the ones who get all the benefits in this country. They're the ones that are always pandered to."[30]
—Rush Limbaugh, radio talk show host

REALITY

The affluent get more from the government than the poor.

Often, their benefits come in the form of tax breaks or exemptions, rather than social spending, but the effects on the budget deficit—and on the amount of cash in people's pockets—are the same.

- In 1992, Uncle Sam spent about $464 billion on entitlements that people receive regardless of their income level, such as Social Security, Medicare, veterans' pensions and retirement, and unemployment insurance benefits. That's about 10 times more than was spent on AFDC and Food Stamps in the same year.[31]

- In 1994, 29% of families with an income of $150,000 or more received government benefits averaging more than $16,000 through programs such as Social Security. Families with incomes of less than $10,000, in contrast, received benefits averaging less than $8,000.[32]

- Children and single parents eligible for Survivors' Benefits through Social Security as the result of the death of a parent or spouse

Ron Barrett

receive about 3 times as much as those who receive AFDC as the result of being abandoned by a parent or spouse. Unlike adults on AFDC, recipients of Survivors' Benefits are not subject to any work requirements or restrictions on ownership of a house or car.[33]

COMPARISON OF EXPENDITURES ON HOUSING, HEALTH CARE, AND CASH TRANSFERS[34]

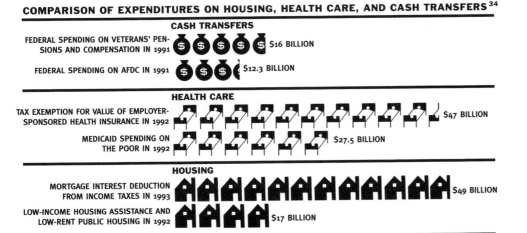

CASH TRANSFERS

FEDERAL SPENDING ON VETERANS' PENSIONS AND COMPENSATION IN 1991 — $16 BILLION

FEDERAL SPENDING ON AFDC IN 1991 — $12.3 BILLION

HEALTH CARE

TAX EXEMPTION FOR VALUE OF EMPLOYER-SPONSORED HEALTH INSURANCE IN 1992 — $47 BILLION

MEDICAID SPENDING ON THE POOR IN 1992 — $27.5 BILLION

HOUSING

MORTGAGE INTEREST DEDUCTION FROM INCOME TAXES IN 1993 — $49 BILLION

LOW-INCOME HOUSING ASSISTANCE AND LOW-RENT PUBLIC HOUSING IN 1992 — $17 BILLION

"They are more pervasive than television in the homes of the elderly, more common than puppies in households with children. They are fixtures in almost half of American families, as familiar as the local letter carrier who delivers them with the daily mail. They are federal entitlements. . . ."[35]

DAVID HAGE, DAVID FISCHER, and ROBERT F. BLACK, journalists

MYTH

"Corporate welfare is anti-business as well as anti-taxpayer."[36]
—Stephen Moore,
The Cato Institute

REALITY

Despite much public criticism, corporate welfare has resisted reform. It enjoys enormous support from a wide range of powerful businesses and special-interest groups.

- The federal government doles out $85 billion yearly in direct subsidy programs to private business, a sum that amounts to about a third of the annual federal budget deficit.[37]

- The total cost of bailing out failed savings and loan associations over a period of about 10 years has been estimated at about $200 billion.[38]

- In 1992, total subsidies to agriculture (including, but not limited to, price supports) amounted to about $29 billion, more than was spent on AFDC.[39]

- Many subsidies contribute to environmental problems. Free road building in national forests helps private timber companies but threatens fragile ecosystems. Federal laws limit the liability of the nuclear power industry in the event of major radiation spills or meltdowns.

Corporations are getting more and more tax breaks.

- The Office of Management and Budget estimates that the cost of tax breaks to corporations and wealthy individuals in fiscal 1996 will be $440 billion, more than 17 times combined state and federal spending on AFDC.[40]

- Today, federal taxes paid by corporations average only about 24% of profits, compared with about 45% in the 1950s.[41]

Paul Corio

- As a result, corporations now account for a much smaller share of tax revenues, leaving individual taxpayers to make up the difference. In 1995, corporate taxes amounted to only 10% of total federal tax revenue, compared with 23% in 1960.[42]

- Corporations now find it much easier to pick up and move in search of lower costs and fewer regulations. As a result, many states and towns are forced to compete with one another in offering generous tax breaks and other subsidies.

CORPORATE TAXES AS A PERCENTAGE OF ALL FEDERAL TAX REVENUE, 1960 AND 1995[43]

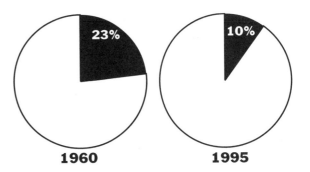

23% — 1960

10% — 1995

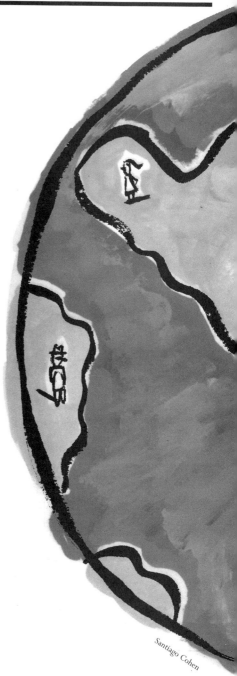

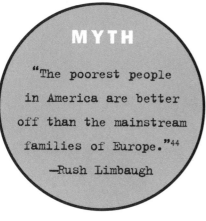

MYTH

"The poorest people in America are better off than the mainstream families of Europe."[44]
—Rush Limbaugh

REALITY

Other industrialized countries do a far better job than we do of alleviating poverty (see graph).

The main reason for lower poverty rates in these countries is simple: Their tax and transfer programs work better than ours.

- In the absence of any government intervention, France, Sweden, and the U.K. would have had much higher poverty rates than the U.S. in the mid-1980s.[45]

- The U.S. devotes a smaller percentage of its GDP to social expenditures than France, Sweden, the U.K., or Germany.[46]

POVERTY RATES IN 5 INDUSTRIALIZED COUNTRIES*[47]

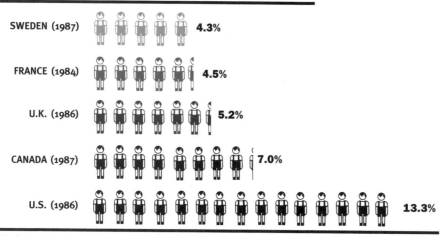

SWEDEN (1987)	4.3%
FRANCE (1984)	4.5%
U.K. (1986)	5.2%
CANADA (1987)	7.0%
U.S. (1986)	13.3%

*For international comparisons, poverty is defined here as family income below 40% of national median income.

Santiago Cohen

UPI/Bettman

The countries of northwestern Europe provide excellent, publicly funded health care for all their citizens.

- They also provide much more support for parents than the U.S. does, in the form of family allowances, publicly subsidized child care, and paid family leaves from work.[48]

See p. 142 for abbreviations used in notes.

1. Ronald Reagan, State of the Union Address, 1/25/1988, *Public Papers of the Presidents, Ronald Reagan,* 1988, p.8, v.1 (Washington, DC: GPO, 1990).

2. Republican Study Committee, *Running from Reality: How Liberals Can't Accept the Failure of the Welfare State,* 5/19/94, p.1.

3. *Money Income and Poverty Status in the U.S., 1989* (CPR, P-60, no. 168), p. 57, Table 19. SA 1994, p. 475, Table 727. Dow Jones News Service, 10/5/95.

4. Carmen D. Solomon, *Aid to Families with Dependent Children (AFDC): Need Standards, Payment Standards, and Maximum Benefits,* Congressional Research Service Report to Congress (Washington, DC, 1/18/95), p. 29.

5. Laurence Mishel and Jared Bernstein, *The State of Working America 1994–95* (Armonk, NY: M.E. Sharpe, 1994). Nancy Folbre and CPE, *The New Field Guide to the U.S. Economy* (New York: The New Press, 1995), pp. 2.5–2.6.

6. Sheldon H. Danziger and Daniel H. Weinberg, "The Historical Record: Trends in Family Income, Inequality, and Poverty," in *Confronting Poverty. Prescriptions for Change,* Sheldon Danziger, Gary D. Sandefur, and Daniel H. Weinberg, ed. (Cambridge: Harvard University Press, 1994).

7. Lewis D. Eigen and Jonathan P. Siegel, eds., *The Macmillan Dictionary of Political Quotations* (New York: Macmillan, 1993), p. 530.

8. Heritage Foundation, *Combatting Family Disintegration, Crime, and Dependence: Welfare Reform and Beyond* (Washington, DC, 4/8/94), p. 6.

9. Quoted in Leonard Larsen, "The Odd Ascent of William Bennett," *Arizona Daily Star,* 12/31/90, p. C1.

10. *Federal Register* 60, no. 27 (2/9/1995), p.7772.

11. Christopher Jencks, *Rethinking Social Policy: Race, Poverty, and the Underclass* (New York: Harper Collins, 1992), p. 209.

12. Patricia Ruggles, *Drawing the Line: Alternative Poverty Measures and Their Implications for Public Policy* (Washington, DC: The Urban Institute Press, 1990).

13. Ruggles, p. 19.

14. Trudi Renwick and Barbara Bergmann, "A Budget-based Definition of Poverty, With an Application to Single-Parent Families," *Journal of Human Resources* 28, no.1 (Winter 1993): pp.1–24.

15. Robert Pear, "A Revised Definition of Poverty May Raise Number of U.S. Poor," *NYT,* 4/30/95, p. A1.

16. Heritage Foundation, p. 1.

17. "The $5.3 Trillion Hype," *WP* 4/10/95, p. A20.

18. Figures for AFDC from *1994 Green Book,* p. 389; figures for Food Stamps from *SA 1994,* pp. 385-6, Tables 601-602. Figures on Medicaid spending on AFDC recipients from *SA 1994,* p. 116, Table 162.

19. Figures for GDP from President's Council of Economic Advisors, *Economic Report of the President 1995* (Washington, DC: GPO), p. 274, Table B1; figures for federal budget from *SA 1994,* p. 332.

20. Same as above.

21. Republican Study Committee, p. 7.

22. Mark Robert Rank, *Living on the Edge: The Realities of Welfare in America* (New York: Columbia University Press, 1994), p. 3.

23. *1994 Green Book,* p. 755, Table 18-1.

24. In 1992, the average monthly benefit per recipient on AFDC was $136; for a 3-person family, that amounts to $4896 per year; see *1994 Green Book,* p. 395, Table 10-24. In the same year, average monthly Food Stamp benefits per person were $68.50; for a 3-person family, that amounts to $2,466; see *1994 Green Book,* p. 782, Table 18-11. Average Medicaid expenditures calculated by dividing total spending on AFDC recipients by total number of AFDC recipients for 1992, SA 1994, p. 116, Table 162.

25. Same as above.

26. Solomon, p. 29.

27. *Poverty in the U.S., 1992* (CPR, P-60, no. 185), p.32, Table 7.

28. *1994 Green Book,* p. 1173.

29. Quoted in Rank, p. 1.

30. Rush Limbaugh, *The Way Things Ought to Be* (New York: Pocket Books, 1993), p. 41.

31. *SA 1994,* p. 372, Table 576; p. 115, Table 159.

32. David Hage, David Fischer, and Robert F. Black, "America's Other Welfare State," *USNWR,* 4/10/95, p. 34.

33. *Social Security Bulletin, Annual Statistical Supplement,* 1993 (Washington, DC: GPO, 1993), Table 9.G1, p. 330, Table 5.F4, p. 223.

34. *SA 1994,* p. 373, Table 577; p. 336, Table 510; p. 371, Table 573; Green Book, p. 802.

35. Hage, Fischer, and Black, p. 34.

36. Stephen Moore, "How to Slash Corporate Welfare," *NYT,* 4/5/95, p. A25.

37. "Go After Corporate Welfare," unsigned editorial, *NYT,* 1/17/95, p. A18.

38. Folbre and the CPE, p. 9.12.

39. Center for Responsive Politics, Washington, DC, 1994.

40. Chuck Collins, "Aid to Dependent Corporations: Exposing Federal Handouts to the Wealthy," *Dollars and Sense,* May-June 1995, p. 15.

41. Folbre and the CPE, p. 5.12.

42. *Budget of the U.S. Government, Historical Tables 1995* (Washington, DC: GPO, 1995), pp. 23–24, Table 2.2; figures for 1995 are estimates.

43. Same as above.

44. Quoted in Steve Rendall, Jim Naurekas, and Jeff Cohen, *The Way Things Aren't: Rush Limbaugh's Reign of Error* (New York: The New Press, 1995), p. 22.

45. Gary Burtless, "Public Spending on the Poor: Historical Trends and Economic Limits," in Danziger, Sandefur, and Weinberg, p. 82; estimates include income and near-cash income minus national taxes.

46. Mishel and Bernstein, p.349.

47. Burtless, p. 81.

48. Norman Ginsburg, *Divisions of Welfare: A Critical Introduction to Comparative Social Policy* (Newbury Park, CA: Sage, 1992); Barbara Bergmann, "European Models of Welfare Reform" (Department of Economics, American University, Washington, DC, manuscript, October 1995).

The
Poor

Thor Swift / Impact Visuals

MYTH

"Welfare recipients are people 'in the wagon' who ought to get out and 'help the rest of us pull.'"[1]
—Senator Phil Gramm, paraphrased by columnist George F. Will

"We simply must abandon the welfare state and move to an opportunity society."[2]
—Newt Gingrich, Speaker of the House of Representatives

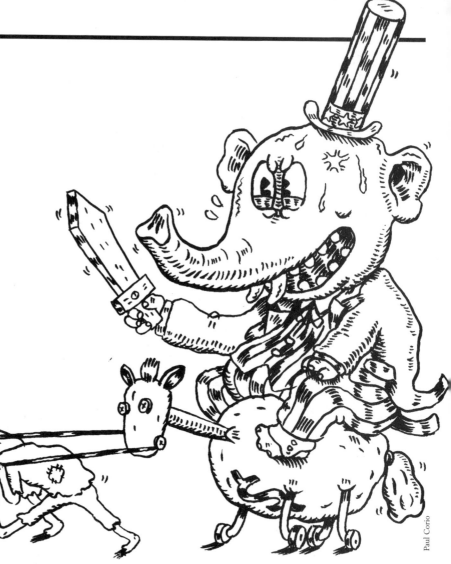

Paul Corio

REALITY

About two-thirds of all AFDC recipients are children. They are not getting much of a ride.

- Children in the U.S. are poorer than children in most other Western industrialized nations because the gap between rich and poor is so large and because welfare programs are less generous here than elsewhere.[3]

Poverty constricts children's opportunities.

- Poor children are more than twice as likely as other children to suffer from stunted growth, severe physical or mental disabilities, fatal accidental injuries, iron deficiency, and severe asthma.[4]

- Poor children are more than twice as likely as other children never to finish high school, even when differences in family structure, race, and ethnicity are taken into account.[5]

- Poor children have significantly lower achievement test scores than children of high-income families.[6]

Poverty rates are extremely high among children of color.

In 1993, 46% of all African-American children and 41% of all Latino children lived in families with incomes below the poverty level.[7]

"That one-fifth of the nation's children, including more than two-thirds of all black children, spend time on welfare by the age of 18 is less an indictment of the welfare system than a symptom of vast social calamity."[9]

ERIK ECKHOLM, journalist

Poverty rates among children have increased since 1970.

POVERTY RATE FOR CHILDREN IN THE U.S.[8]

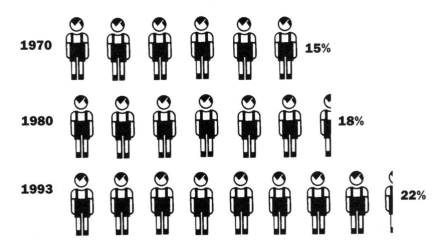

1970   15%

1980   18%

1993   22%

> **MYTH** "Both AFDC and Food Stamps flout the work ethic, offering support to able-bodied Americans whether they work or not—the only major components of our "welfare state" that do this. Social Security's retirement benefits, in contrast, go only to workers."[10]
> —Mickey Kaus

REALITY

Social Security benefits go to many individuals who have never worked for pay, which helps explain why they have effectively improved the overall standard of living in the U.S.

- In 1992, more than 20% of all benefits paid through Social Security went to spouses or children of retired or disabled workers.[11]

- In 1991, almost as much federal money was spent on Social Security Survivor's Benefits to children of deceased workers as was spent on AFDC ($12.5 billion versus $14 billion).[12]

- Generous funding of Social Security has successfully reduced poverty among elders. Between 1967 and 1985, the real value of Social Security benefits rose 233%; the real value of AFDC fell 37%.[13]

Poverty rates are now much lower among elders than among children (see graph).

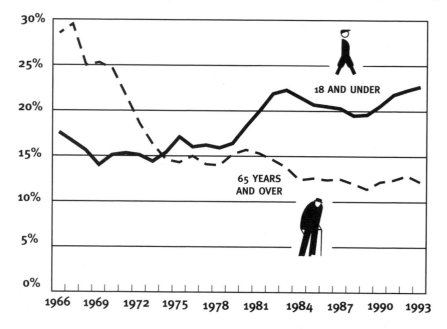

POVERTY RATE FOR PERSONS UNDER 18 AND 65 YEARS AND OLDER (ALL RACES)[14]

Christopher Smith / Impact Visuals

The benefits of Social Security are unevenly distributed.

- The average retiree receives far more than he or she paid into the system, regardless of family income or level of need.[15]

- Elderly women and people of color remain particularly vulnerable to poverty. In 1993, 24% of all women 65 had incomes under 125% of the poverty level, compared with 13% of men in that age group.[16]

- In the same year, 28% of African-Americans and 21% of Latinos over age 65 were poor, compared with 11% of whites.[17]

MYTH

"Every threat to
the fabric of this
country—from poverty to
homelessness—is connected
to out-of-wedlock teen
pregnancy."[18]
—Jonathan Alter,
journalist

"If we are talking about
13- and 14-year-olds,
the answer is to stop
sleeping around. . . .
What is needed is not
a new government program,
but a new ethos—one in
which these little girls
will be encouraged to
keep their knees together
until they grow up and
find husbands."[19]
—Midge Decter,
conservative activist

REALITY

Births to teen mothers are not the primary cause of poverty.

- Many teen mothers live in poor families in poor neighborhoods and have access only to poor schools. A study controlling for these factors by comparing girls from the same family found that those who postponed pregnancy were not significantly more likely to finish high school, get married, or escape poverty than sisters who bore children during their teen years.[20]

- In 1992, 42% of families on AFDC included children who had been born to a teenage mother, but this percentage has remained about the same for the last 20 years.[21]

Teen mothers are a relatively small group.

- In 1993, about 7% of mothers were unwed teenagers. Their kids represented less than 1% of all related children living in families.[22]

- Only about 8% of all welfare households are headed by teen mothers.[23]

Births among unwed teens reflect larger social trends.

- Teen birth rates are declining. In 1970, there were about 68 births per 1,000 teenage women; by 1990, there were about 60. The percentage born out of wedlock has increased because marriage has become less common.[24]

- Out-of-wedlock births have increased among all age and income groups. Between 1982 and 1992, birthrates for unmarried mothers increased faster among women ages 20 to 39 than among teenagers.[25]

Young women are not the only ones responsible.

- More than two-thirds of teen mothers are impregnated by men over age 20.[26] A majority of teen mothers have experienced rape or other sexual abuse.[27]

- Teenage women living in poverty are less likely than those from higher-income families to obtain an abortion if they become pregnant, partly because they have less access to abortion. About 39% of those living in poverty, compared with about 70% of those in higher-income families, terminate unplanned pregnancies.[28]

Russell Christian

MYTH

"It's unfair that hard-working people have to support immigrants through the welfare system."[29]
—Ariana Huffington, California socialite

"My ancestors, and most of our ancestors, came to this country not with their hands out for welfare checks."[30]
—Rep. Bill Archer, R-Texas

REALITY

Overall, immigrants pay more in taxes than they receive from government programs.

- Between 1970 and 1994, immigrants generated a net public-sector surplus of more than $25 billion annually.[31]

- Legal immigrants are prohibited from receiving most forms of public assistance until 3 to 5 years after arrival.

- Illegal immigrants are not, and never have been, eligible for cash welfare payments or Food Stamps. They have legal rights to public education and medical treatment at a public hospital, though these rights were recently challenged by California's Proposition 187.

- An Immigration and Naturalization Service study released in 1992 found that less than 0.5% of illegal immigrants had fraudulently obtained Food Stamps or AFDC payments.[32]

Historically, immigrants to the U.S. (including most of our ancestors) have enjoyed the benefits of a social safety net.

- In the early 1900s, first-generation immigrant families were 3 times more likely than other immigrant families to receive assistance, and they accounted for about one-third of all those in public hospitals.[33]

The costs and benefits of immigration are unequally distributed.

- States and municipalities often pay the costs imposed by immigrants; the federal government collects the taxes paid by immigrants.

- Employers benefit the most. Workers who are afraid of being deported can be paid subminimum wages and exposed to dangerous working conditions.

Peter Kelly / Impact Visuals

MYTH "The biggest dietary problem of people living in poverty is obesity, not hunger."[34]
—Robert Rector, The Heritage Foundation

REALITY

Many children living in poverty don't get enough to eat.

- Low-income children are not more obese than children from more affluent homes. However, they are more likely to have stunted growth because of malnutrition.[35]

F.M. Kearney / Impact Visuals

- About 4 million children under age 12 live in households without sufficient food.[36] One-third to one-half of impoverished children consume significantly less than the federally recommended level of calories and nutrients needed for normal learning and thinking.[37]

Inadequacies in food assistance programs mean that many poor people go hungry.

- More than half of all Food Stamp recipients are children.[38]

- When the U.S. Conference of Mayors met in December 1994, they found that requests for food assistance had risen 12% during the year, along with requests for emergency shelter. Shelters in 72% of the cities represented at the meeting turned away requests for assistance because of lack of resources.[39]

- Second Harvest, the nation's largest network of private hunger-relief agencies, reports turning away 61,000 people each year for lack of food.[40]

- An Urban Institute study in 1993 estimated that about 16% of people age 60 and older are either hungry or malnourished to some degree, often because they are too poor or too infirm to shop or cook.[41]

MYTH "We have the best health care in the world—despite all the alarm that has been raised about it in the past few years."[42]   —Newt Gingrich

"There was no health-care crisis in this country, at least not until Hillary got her mitts on health care."[43]   —Rush Limbaugh

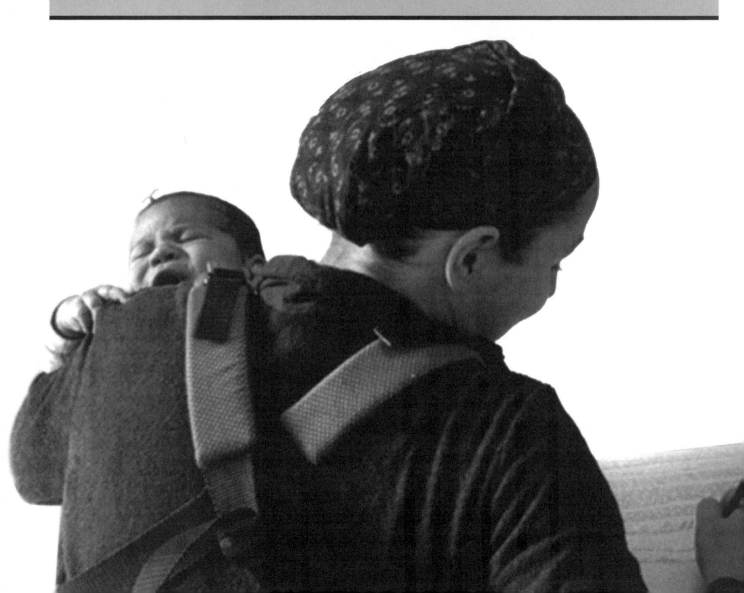

Sue Mell

REALITY

Health care delivery in the U.S. is excellent for some but terrible for others. Though we have some of the best high-tech medical facilities in the world, many people lack access to them. Infant mortality rates are lower in 21 other countries, including Canada, Germany, and Japan. Infant mortality rates are higher among African-American children than in 40 other nations, including Sri Lanka, Malaysia, and Cuba.[44]

The number of Americans who lack health insurance is growing. In 1993, 17% of the population under age 65 lacked health insurance, up from 13% in 1980.[45]

Many low-income families cannot afford health insurance. In 1993, 35% of all Americans under age 65 with family incomes of less than $16,000 lacked health insurance, compared with only 5% for those with family incomes of $50,000 or more.[46] More and more employers are reducing health insurance benefits for their employees.[47]

Racial and ethnic inequalities in health insurance access are

large. Among people under age 65, 34% of all Latinos and 23% of all African-Americans lacked health insurance, compared with 16% of all whites.[48] A large percentage of Latinos live in the South and West, regions where the workforce is less unionized and employers are less likely to provide health care benefits.

Individuals without health care insurance are often unable to obtain adequate medical care.

- Although the Medicare system covers all people age 65 and over, Medicaid provides assistance for only about half of the poor.[49]

- Many public hospitals are being closed down. State and federal laws require all hospitals to provide care to the uninsured in medical emergencies, but only public hospitals are obligated to treat them in other situations.[50]

- In 1991, uninsured patients had death rates significantly higher than privately insured patients.[51]

George Cohen / Impact Visuals

MYTH "You could abolish Housing and Urban Development (HUD) tomorrow morning, and improve life in most of America."[52]
—Newt Gingrich

REALITY

This country has a shortage of affordable housing.

- Fewer families can now afford to buy their own homes. The home ownership rate for individuals ages 30 to 34 fell from 57% in 1980 to 51% in 1993.[54]

- Demand for emergency shelter services has intensified over the past 10 years.[55]

- In 1994, families with children accounted for about 39% of the homeless population, up from about 27% in 1985.[56]

Federal housing assistance provided through HUD has helped many low-income families but has never been sufficiently funded.

- Of 13.8 million low-income renter households eligible for federal housing assistance, almost 10 million receive no help at all.[57]

- Rental housing assistance to low-income persons has declined from $69 billion in 1977 to $17 billion in 1995, in inflation-adjusted dollars.[58]

Most federal housing assistance today goes to the affluent, not the poor (see graph).

WHERE GOVERNMENT HOUSING SUBSIDIES WENT IN 1993[59]

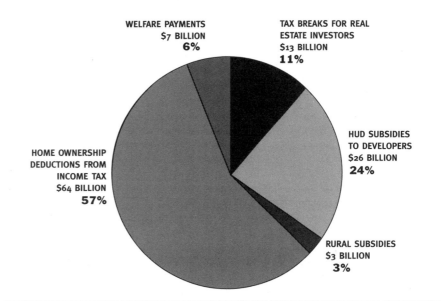

WELFARE PAYMENTS
$7 BILLION
6%

TAX BREAKS FOR REAL ESTATE INVESTORS
$13 BILLION
11%

HUD SUBSIDIES TO DEVELOPERS
$26 BILLION
24%

HOME OWNERSHIP DEDUCTIONS FROM INCOME TAX
$64 BILLION
57%

RURAL SUBSIDIES
$3 BILLION
3%

"A review of recent figures from Congress' Joint Taxation Committee shows that 44% of last year's $51 billion homeowner subsidy went to the richest 5% of tax-payers—those with incomes of more than $100,000. Only one-fifth of middle-class tax-payers—the 28 million households with incomes between $30,000 and $50,000—received any mortgage subsidy."[60]

PETER DREIER and **JOHN ATLAS**, journalists

Russell Christian

See p. 142 for abbreviations used in notes.

1. George F. Will, "Reformers Would Compound the Tragedy of Welfare," *BG*, 9/15/95, p. 31.
2. Newt Gingrich, *To Renew America* (New York: HarperCollins, 1995), p. 9.
3. Keith Bradsher, "Low Ranking for Poor American Children," *NYT*, 8/14/95, p. A9.
4. *The State of America's Children Yearbook 1995* (Washington, DC: Children's Defense Fund, 1995), p. 19.
5. *The State of America's Children*, p. 20.
6. *Wasting America's Future: The Children's Defense Fund Report on the Costs of Child Poverty* (Boston: Beacon Press, 1994), p. 79.
7. *The State of America's Children*, p. 101.
8. *The State of America's Children*, p. 18.
9. Erik Eckholm, "Solutions on Welfare: They All Cost Money," *NYT*, 7/26/92, p. 1.
10. Mickey Kaus, "They Blew It," *New Republic*, 12/5/94, p. 18.
11. *1994 Green Book*, p. 34, Table 1-15.
12. *Social Security Bulletin, Annual Statistical Supplement, 1993* (Washington, DC: GPO 1993), Table 9.G1, p. 330; Table 5.F4, p. 223.
13. Barbara Wolfe, "The Deteriorating Economic Circumstances of Children," in *Essays on the Economics of Discrimination,* ed. Emily Hoffman (Kalamazoo, MI: W.E. Upjohn Institute for Employment Research, 1991), p. 55.
14. *Income, Poverty, and Valuation of Noncash Benefits: 1993* (CPR, P-60, no. 188), p. D-17, Table D-5.
15. Robert D. Hershey, Jr., "Misunderstanding Social Security," *NYT*, 8/20/95, p. E4.
16. *Income, Poverty, and Valuation of Noncash Benefits: 1993*, p. 22, Table 8.
17. Retrieved electronically from Census Bureau Current Population Survey, March 1994. Table 3.
18. Jonathan Alter, "The Name of the Game Is Shame: The New Reactionaries Are Those Who Excuse Teen Pregnancy," *Newsweek*, 12/12/94, p. 41.
19. Midge Decter, "Sex and God in American Politics: What Conservatives Really Think," *Policy Review* (Summer 1984), p. 23.
20. Arline T. Geronimus and Sanders Korenman, "The Socioeconomic Consequences of Teen Childbearing Reconsidered," *Quarterly Journal of Economics* 107, no. 4 (1992), pp. 1187–1214. See also Greg J. Duncan and Saul D. Hoffman, "Welfare Benefits, Economic Opportunities, and Out-of-Wedlock Births Among Black Teenage Girls," *Demography* 27, no. 4 (November 1990), pp. 519–35.
21. GAO, *Families on Welfare: Teenage Mothers Least Likely to Be Self-Sufficient* (Washington, DC, May 1994).
22. Center on Hunger, Poverty, and Nutrition Policy, *Statement on Key Welfare Reform Issues: The Empirical Evidence* (Medford, MA: Tufts University, 1995), p. 20.
23. Diana Pearce and Emily Knearl, *Teen Pregnancy, Welfare, and Poverty* (Washington, DC: Wider Opportunities for Women, 1994).
24. *SA 1994*, p. 76, Table 92.
25. Center on Hunger, Poverty, and Nutrition Policy, p. 21.
26. Mark Males, "Why Blame Young Girls?" *NYT*, 7/29/94, p. A27.
27. Center for Law and Social Policy, "Marriage v. Money: Family Structure, Income, and Welfare Reform," *Family Matters* 7, nos. 2 and 3 (Spring, Summer 1995), p. 16.
28. Alan Guttmacher Institute, *Teen-Age Pregnancy and the Welfare Reform Debate: Issues in Brief* (Washington, DC: February 1995).
29. "Firing Line Debates Immigration," *The Jerome Levy Economics Institute Report* 5, no. 4 (August 1995), p. 3.
30. Quoted in Frederick Rose, "The Growing Backlash Against Immigration Includes Many Myths," *WSJ*, 4/26/95, p. A1.
31. Michael Fix and Jeffrey S. Passel, "Balancing the Ledger on Jobs, Taxes," *LAT*, 8/2/94, p. B7. See also Michael Fix and Jeffrey S. Passel, *Immigrants and Immigration: Setting the Record Straight* (Washington, DC: The Urban Institute Press, 1994).
32. Steve Rendall, Jim Naurekas, and Jeff Cohen, *The Way Things Aren't: Rush Limbaugh's Reign of Error* (New York: The New Press, 1995), p. 47.
33. Rose, p. A1.
34. Quoted in Richard Saltus, "Bad Diets Hamper the Poor," *BG*, 5/3/95, p. A3.
35. Saltus, p. A3.
36. Barbara Vobejda, "4 Million U.S. Children Under 12 Go Hungry at Home, Study Says," *WP*, 7/20/95, p. A4.
37. Saltus, p. A3.
38. *The State of America's Children 1995*, p. 45.
39. Guy Gugliotta, "Hunger and Homelessness on the Rise, Mayors Warn," *WP*, 12/20/94, p. A8.
40. *The State of America's Children*, p. 46.
41. Michael J. McCarthy, "Hunger Among Elderly Surges: Meal Programs Just Can't Keep Up," *WSJ*, 11/8/94, p. A1.
42. Gingrich, p. 176.
43. Rush Limbaugh, *See, I Told You So* (New York: Pocket Books, 1993), p. 168.
44. *The State of America's Children*, p. 28.
45. U.S. Department of Health and Human Services, *Health U.S. 1994 Chartbook* (Washington, DC: GPO, 1994), p. 35.
46. *Health U.S.1994 Chartbook*, p. 35.
47. *The State of America's Children*, p. 28.
48. *Health U.S.1994 Chartbook*, p. 35.
49. *Poverty in the U.S., 1992* (CPR, P-60, no. 185), p. 32, Table 7.
50. Kevin Sack, "Public Hospitals Around Country Cut Basic Service," *NYT*, 8/20/95, p. A1.
51. Robert Lavelle and the Staff of Blackside, *America's New War on Poverty* (San Francisco: KQED Books, 1995), p. 143.
52. Quoted in Peter Dreier and John Atlas, "Housing Policy's Moment of Truth," *The American Prospect* (Summer 1995), p. 73.
53. Rush Limbaugh, *The Way Things Ought to Be* (New York: Pocket Books, 1993), p. 256.
54. Dreier and Atlas, p. 70. *SA 1994*, p. 740, Table 1220.
55. Dreier and Atlas, p. 70.
56. *The State of America's Children*, p. 63. Nancy Folbre and the CPE, *The New Field Guide to the U.S. Economy* (New York: The New Press, 1995), p. 6.12.
57. Dreier and Atlas, p. 71.
58. *The State of America's Children*, p. 66.
59. Dreier and Atlas, p. 70; Pentagon subsidies to house military personnel, about $10 billion annually, are not included.
60. Peter Dreier and John Atlas, "Mansions on the Hill," *In These Times*, June 26-July 9, 1995, p. 22.

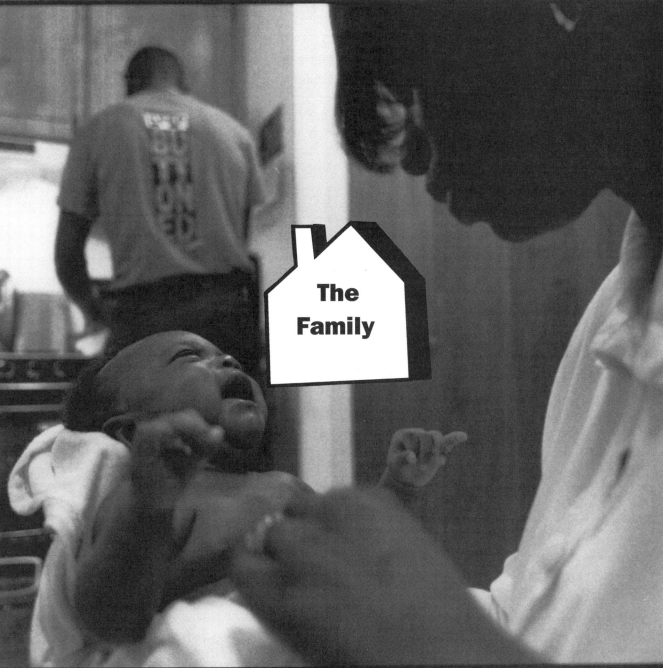

The
Family

Linda Rosier / Impact Visuals

MYTH

"Scientific research confirms that welfare benefits to single mothers directly contribute to the rise in illegitimate births."[1]
—The Heritage Foundation, conservative think tank

"We must remove the enormous economic subsidy for people to form families that are dysfunctional."[2]
—Rep. Jim Talent, R-Missouri

REALITY

Scientific research shows that welfare does not significantly increase out-of-wedlock births.

- In June 1994, 76 prominent researchers in the areas of poverty, the labor market, and family structure signed a statement asserting that research does not support recent suggestions that welfare is the main cause of rising out-of-wedlock births. The signers represent a variety of major institutions, disciplines, and political viewpoints; they include nearly all the major researchers in the field.[3]

Lowering benefit levels will not reduce out-of-wedlock births.

- New Jersey's benefit package is 58% higher than Mississippi's; yet rates of single parenthood in these two states are the same. Mississippi and Alabama have the lowest AFDC benefit levels in the nation, but their teen birthrates are among the highest.[4]

- The value of cash benefits plus Food Stamps has declined over the same period that out-of-wedlock births have increased.

- In the mid-1980s, Canada's public assistance programs for poor single mothers provided benefits about twice as high as those in the U.S, but out-of-wedlock birthrates there remained far lower.[5]

Out-of-wedlock births have increased among all women, not just among those eligible for AFDC.

- Women of all income groups are less likely to marry and stay married than they were 30 years ago. The birthrate among single women has changed very little. But because single women are now a larger percentage of all women, births to single women are a larger percentage of all births.[6]

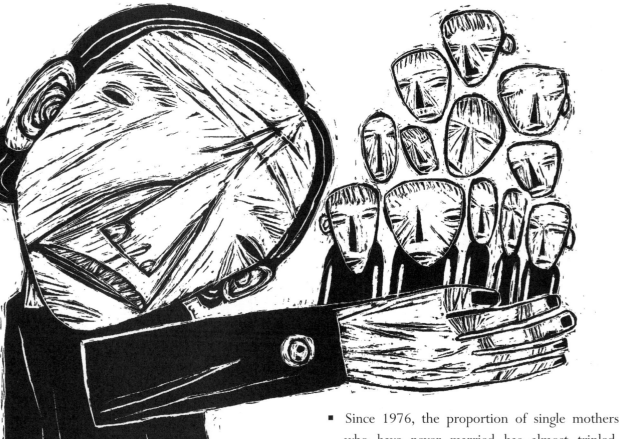

Melinda Beck

- Since 1976, the proportion of single mothers who have never married has almost tripled, increasing to about 36% in 1992.[7]

"We have to recognize that government programs are not the primary cause of the growth in single parenting, and changes in government programs are likely to have only small effects, with potentially large costs."[8]

REBECCA BLANK, economist

MYTH

"No other civilized nation in the world pays young girls to have babies. But that's what our welfare system does."[9]
—Rep. Marge Roukema, R—New Jersey

"Recent evidence from a carefully monitored New Jersey state experiment shows that limiting the value of welfare benefits can have a dramatic impact in reducing illegitimate births among women on welfare."[10]
—Robert Rector, The Heritage Foundation

REALITY

Robert Rector and others jumped to the wrong conclusion regarding the effects of New Jersey's 1992 decision to exclude children born to mothers on welfare from eligibility for benefits.

- A Rutgers University study that took into account time lags in reporting new births found no reduction in the birthrate of welfare mothers attributable to the new child exclusion law.[11]

Welfare recipients don't have more children than other mothers.

- AFDC families average fewer than 2 children.[12]

- Receipt of welfare does not encourage pregnancy. In fact, the longer a woman remains on AFDC, the less likely she is to give birth.[13]

- AFDC families tend to be largest in states with the lowest grant levels, such as Mississippi and Alabama.[14]

Mothers do not "profit" from additional children.

- The difference between the maximum AFDC benefit for a 2-person family and a 3-person family averaged only $72 a month in 1994. In most Southern states, it was far lower.[15]

- The value of the dependent exemption provided by the U.S. income tax code to families with an income over $50,000 is about $57 a month.[16] No one has suggested that this benefit encourages more births among the affluent.

Many pregnancies experienced by women receiving AFDC are partly a result of poverty.

- Low-income women have a hard time getting adequate health care, including contraceptive services.[17]

"The economic, social, and psychological situation in which women on welfare find themselves is simply not conducive to desiring more children. Such women would appear to be motivated by cost-benefit considerations, but it is the costs that outweigh the benefits, not the reverse. Becoming pregnant and having a child are perceived as making the situation worse, not better."[18]

MARK RANK, sociologist

MYTH

"A stronger sense of shame about illegitimacy and divorce would do more than any tax cut, or any new government program, to improve the life circumstances of children."[19]

—David Blankenhorn, Institute for American Values

REALITY

Poverty and public stigma hurt children far more than their mother's marital status.

- Claims regarding the ill effects of divorce on children are all based on a comparison with children in all 2-parent homes. They do not take into account how poorly children of divorce might have fared had their parents remained together in a loveless, angry, or even violent marriage.[20]

- Low income is the single most important factor accounting for the difficulties experienced by children from mother-only families.[21]

Poverty and unemployment make marriage and family life more difficult.

- Poor 2-parent families are about twice as likely to break up as are 2-parent families that aren't poor.[22]

- African-American men are more likely than white men to die or to be sent to prison at a young age. They are also less likely than white men to earn sufficient income to support a family.[23]

"Good" and "bad" families cannot be defined simply in demographic terms. The quality of relationships matters most for children's well-being.

- Many families that conform to the traditional family model suffer from domestic violence or child neglect. Over the 1980s, an average of 1,500 women died each year as a result of domestic violence.[24]

- The majority of women receiving public assistance have been sexually or physically abused as adults. AFDC makes it possible for many women to escape abusive relationships.[25]

Russell Christian

- Poverty, more than any particular family structure, increases the incidence of child abuse.[26]

"Now, Bob Dole made his ex-wife a single mom, Newt Gingrich made his ex-wife a single mom, and Phil Gramm made his ex-wife just an ex-wife, but this is something they all devoutly believe poor people should not do."[27]

MOLLY IVINS, journalist

Laurent Cilluffo

MYTH

"The current welfare system destroys families. . . ."[28]
—Rep. Bill Archer, R-Texas

"In a truly free 'lifestyle market,' marriage will always win. It is divorce, illegitimacy, and cohabitation that require subsidy from the state to survive."[29]
—John Ashcroft, The Rockford Institute

REALITY

Changes in the structure of family life are the result of economic development and change.

- Over the past 200 years or more, economic activity has moved outside the home, and more people have begun to work for individual wages. Children go to school longer and are less likely to contribute to parental income when they grow up.

- As the cost of raising children has increased, fathers have become less willing to fulfill their responsibilities to them. Women have gained political rights and greater economic independence; the family has become more egalitarian but less stable. Elders have become more vulnerable to poverty, and mothers have been forced to pay an increasing share of the costs of raising children. Welfare programs emerged largely as a response to these problems.[30]

Family structure is changing in most countries regardless of national welfare policies.

- The percentage of children living with mothers but not with fathers is particularly high in the developing nations of Latin America, the Caribbean, and sub-Saharan Africa, even though public assistance to the poor is virtually nonexistent in these countries.[31]

- Divorce rates are increasing in most developed countries and are higher in the U.S. than in countries with far more extensive welfare programs.[32]

- International data show a global trend toward an increasing proportion of mother-supported families. This trend has been more rapid in the U.S. than in either Sweden or France, which provide far more generous support for mothers on their own.

SINGLE-PARENT HOUSEHOLDS AS A PERCENTAGE OF ALL HOUSEHOLDS WITH DEPENDENT CHILDREN[33]

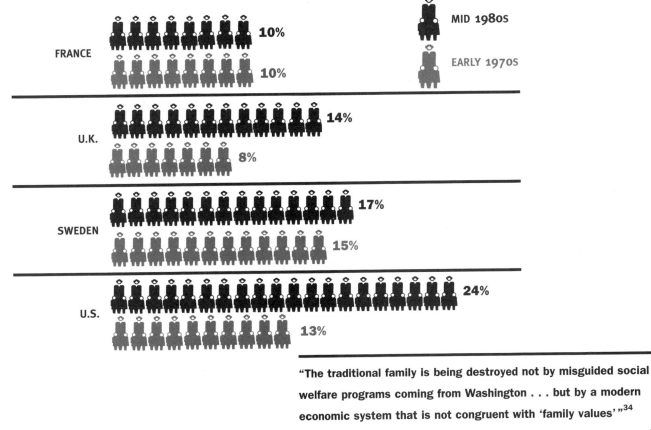

FRANCE 10% / 10%

MID 1980S
EARLY 1970S

U.K. 14% / 8%

SWEDEN 17% / 15%

U.S. 24% / 13%

"The traditional family is being destroyed not by misguided social welfare programs coming from Washington . . . but by a modern economic system that is not congruent with 'family values' "[34]

LESTER THUROW, economist

Paul Corio

MYTH

"In a free society a man cannot long be made to work to pay for children whom he rarely sees, kept by a woman who is living with someone else."[35]
—George Gilder, writer

REALITY

A free society should not be defined as one in which mothers' child-rearing services are free.

- As the costs of child rearing have increased, the tendency of fathers to default on their parental responsibilities has also increased. But most Northern European countries have developed methods of effectively enforcing child support laws. In Sweden, 90% of sums owed are typically collected.[36]

Many rich fathers, as well as poor ones, are deadbeats.

- In the U.S. in 1991, only 56% of custodial mothers were awarded child support payments, and only half of these received the full amount due. This represented only a slight improvement from 1981, when about 47% of those awarded payments received the full amount due.[37]

- About 38% of custodial mothers asked a government agency for assistance in collecting child support in 1991. These agencies were able to collect only one-quarter of what absent parents (primarily fathers) owed.[38]

- A survey of divorced fathers in Denver found that two-thirds spent less on child support than on their monthly car payments. Though most kept their car payments up-to-date, more than half were delinquent in their child support.[39]

Improved child support enforcement would reduce but not eliminate poverty.

- Public assistance is a necessary complement to improved child support enforcement. According to Irwin Garfinkel, a researcher at the University of Wisconsin, "If we had a perfect system and collected 100% of the child support, we would still only cut welfare by 25%."[40]

- Under current rules, mothers on AFDC receive only the first $50 of a father's child support payments. The rest goes to the state to "reimburse" welfare payments.

- Taking fathers' responsibilities seriously would mean providing employment for those who cannot otherwise pay child support.

"It is as though a husband's economic support is in 'payment' for the wife's housekeeping, emotional support, and sexual access, not for her child-rearing activities."[41]

DIANA PEARCE, sociologist

Connie Grosch / Impact Visuals

MYTH

"Despite the widespread perception of difficulties, most mothers find child care fairly easy to arrange. . . . The problem is probably not that care is unavailable, but that these [disadvantaged] mothers have not looked for it."[42]
—Lawrence Mead, political scientist

REALITY

Difficulty finding affordable child care makes it hard for many mothers to work.

- Good infant care is particularly hard to find. Even when it is available, child care schedules don't always fit with job schedules. About 30% of nonworking mothers report they would work if acceptable child care were available.[43]

- Reducing child care costs increases the likelihood that mothers will work outside the home. Recent estimates suggest that providing a full child care subsidy could increase the proportion of poor mothers who work from 29% to 44%.[44]

- In 1990, employed-mother families with a preschool child spent about $275 a month on child care, more than a minimum-wage earner brings home in a week.[45]

Better-quality child care is needed, but it is expensive.

- Recent studies suggest that the average quality of child care is poor to mediocre.[46]

- Head Start, a part-day, part-year program of educational enrichment as well as child care, costs about $310 per child per month. A high-quality full-day program would cost closer to $525 per child per month.[47]

Proposed cuts in federal child care services would make life even more difficult for working parents.

- The child care block grant under consideration in 1995 proposed ending the guarantee of child care assistance for AFDC families, ending requirements that states enforce minimal health and safety standards for publicly funded child care, and reducing food subsidies for child care programs.[48]

Connie Grosch / Impact Visuals

MYTH

"If unwed teenage mothers, cut off from public assistance, are unable to support their children, America should tell them 'We'll help you with foster care, we'll help you with orphanages, we'll help you with adoption'—but not with the cash that might keep mother and child together."[49]
—Time's David van Biema, paraphrasing Newt Gingrich

"Those who find the word 'orphanages' objectionable may think of them as 24-hour-a-day preschools."[50]
—Charles Murray, journalist

fare will make it impossible for many mothers to care for their own children. Many will be forced to relinquish custody to the state.

Separating children from parents simply because of poverty is wrong and doesn't work.

Social scientists find that a strong, stable relationship with a primary caregiver is the single most important determinant of healthy child development.[51]

REALITY

Conservatives have now learned not to use the "o-word," which created a furor in 1994. But restrictions and time limits on wel-

AVERAGE COST OF CARING FOR 1 CHILD FOR 1 YEAR ($1994)[52]

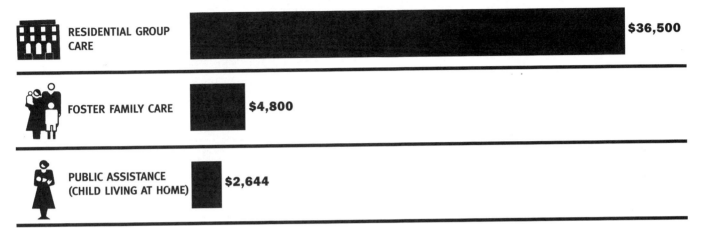

RESIDENTIAL GROUP CARE	$36,500
FOSTER FAMILY CARE	$4,800
PUBLIC ASSISTANCE (CHILD LIVING AT HOME)	$2,644

Harvey Finkle / Impact Visuals

The current orphanage/foster care system cannot accommodate many more children.
About 10 million children receive AFDC.[53] Approximately 630,000 children live with unwed mothers under 18. Institutional care currently accommodates only about 450,000 children.[54]

As of early 1995, 20 states were either under court order to meet federal standards regarding the health and safety of children in foster care or had been sued for failing to meet those standards.[55]

"There's all this talk about family values and now they're talking about splitting up families. It's very contradictory."[56]

JOHNNIE MELTON, director of two group homes in Chicago

See p. 142 for abbreviations used in notes.

1. Heritage Foundation, *Combatting Family Disintegration, Crime and Dependence: Welfare Reform and Beyond* (Washington, DC, 4/8/94), p. 6.
2. "GOP Raises Ax on Welfare," *Boston Herald*, 4/29/94, p. 3.
3. University of Michigan, School of Social Work, Research and Training Program on Poverty, the Underclass, and Public Policy, press release, June 23, 1994.
4. Center on Budget and Policy Priorities, *Out-of-Wedlock Childbearing and Welfare Reform* (Washington, DC, 1995); Jared Bernstein, "Welfare-Bashing Redux: The Return of Charles Murray," *The Humanist*, 55, no. 1 (January/February 1995), pp. 22–25.
5. Rebecca Blank, "What Are the Trends in Nonmarital Births?," in *Looking Before We Leap: Social Science and Welfare Reform*, ed. R. Kent Weaver and William T. Dickens (Washington, DC: Brookings Institution, 1995), p. 31.
6. Blank, p. 28.
7. GAO, Report to the Chairman, Subcommittee on Human Resources, Committee on Ways and Means, House of Representatives, *Families on Welfare: Sharp Rise in Never-Married Women Reflects Societal Trend* (Washington, DC: GPO, May 1994), p. 17.
8. Rebecca Blank, "Unwed Mothers Need Role Models, Not Roll Backs, " *WSJ*, 3/7/95, p. A18.
9. *Congressional Digest*, June-July 1995, p. 184.
10. Robert Rector, *FYI* (Heritage Foundation newsletter), 2/9/95.
11. Michael C. Laracy, "'If It Seems Too Good to Be True, It Probably Is,' Observations on Rutgers University's Initial Evaluation Findings That New Jersey's Child Exclusion Law Has Not Reduced AFDC Birth Rates," Report, Annie E. Casey Foundation, June 21, 1995. For further information, contact Professor Michael J. Camasso, School of Social Work, Rutgers University, New Brunswick, NJ 08903.
12. *1994 Green Book*, p. 401, Table 10-27.
13. Mark Rank, *Living on the Edge. The Realities of Welfare in America* (New York: Columbia University Press, 1994), p. 76.
14. National Abortion and Reproductive Rights Action League, "Welfare Reform and Child Exclusion Laws," p. 2.
15. *1994 Green Book*, pp. 368-69, Table 10-12.
16. In the 28% tax bracket, the $2,450 dependent deduction is worth about $686 in tax savings.
17. National Abortion and Reproductive Rights Action League, p. 3.
18. Rank, pp. 77–78.
19. Cited in Caryl Rivers, "The New Puritanism," *BG*, 3/8/95, p. 19.
20. Judith Stacey, "The New Family Values Crusaders," *The Nation*, July 25/August 1, 1994, pp. 119–21. See also Frank F. Furstenberg, Jr., and Andrew J. Cherlin, *Divided Families: What Happens to Children When Parents Part* (Cambridge: Harvard University Press, 1991).
21. Sara S. McLanahan, "The Consequences of Single Motherhood," *The American Prospect* 18 (Summer 1994), pp. 48–58.
22. *Studies in Household and Family Formation* (CPR, P-23, no. 179), pp. 29–30.
23. Christopher Farrell and Karen Pennar, "Welfare Reform Won't Patch Up Poor Families," *Business Week*, 1/23/95, p. 78.
24. Barbara Vobejda, "Allegations Focus National Attention on Society's Response to Drug Abuse," *WP*, 6/19/94, p. A18.
25. IWPR, *Measuring the Costs of Domestic Violence and the Cost Effectiveness of Interventions* (Washington, DC: May 31, 1995); Jody Raphael, *Domestic Violence: Telling the Untold Welfare-to-Work Story* (Chicago: The Taylor Institute, January 1995).
26. Arloc Sherman, *Wasting America's Future: The Children's Defense Fund Report on the Costs of Child Poverty* (Boston: Beacon Press, 1994), pp. 33–39, 62.
27. Molly Ivins, "Illegitimacy Ratio—Another Idiotic GOP Policy," *Liberal Opinion Week*, 3/27/95, p. 4.
28. Quoted in *Congressional Digest*, June-July 1995, p. 174.
29. John Ashcroft, "The Family and the Welfare State," *Vital Speeches of the Day* 56, no. 19 (July 15, 1995), p. 599.
30. Nancy Folbre, *Who Pays for the Kids? Gender and the Structures of Constraint* (New York: Routledge, 1994).
31. Judith Bruce, Cynthia Lloyd, and Ann Leonard, *Families in Focus: New Perspectives on Mothers, Fathers, and Children* (New York: Population Council, 1995), p. 79.
32. Bruce, Lloyd, and Leonard, p. 20, Table 10.
33. Bruce, Lloyd, and Leonard, p. 18, Table 8; figures pertain to households with at least 1 resident parent.
34. Lester Thurow, "Companies Merge: Families Break Up," *NYT*, 9/3/95, p. E11.
35. George Gilder, *Wealth and Poverty* (New York: Basic Books, 1981), p. 115.
36. Mary Ann Glendon, *The Transformation of Family Law: State, Law, and Family in the United States and Western Europe* (Chicago: University of Chicago Press, 1989), pp. 197–238.
37. Census Bureau Press Release, Department of Health and Human Services, May 13, 1995; *Child Support for Custodial Mothers and Fathers: 1991* (CPR, P-60, no. 187). *SA 1993*, p. 385, Table 611.
38. "Child Support Money Is Up but Far Short," *NYT*, 1/7/94, p. A14.
39. Steven A. Holmes, "Day Care Bill Marks a Turn Toward Help for the Poor," *NYT*, 4/8/90, p. E4.
40. Rick Bragg, *"Georgia, Passing Child Support, Discovers Its Potential and Limits"*, *NYT*, 4/14/95, p. A1.
41. Diana Pearce, "Women, Work and Welfare: The Feminization of Poverty," in *Working Women and Their Families*, ed. Karen Wolk Feinstein (London: Sage Publications, 1992), p. 122.
42. Lawrence Mead, *The New Politics of Poverty: The Nonworking Poor in America* (New York: Basic Books, 1992), pp. 122–23.
43. Rebecca Maynard, "Framing the Federal Child Care Debate: Realities and Myths," *Jobs and Capital* 4 (Winter 1995), p. 46.
44. GAO, Report to the Congressional Caucus for Women's Issues, *Child Care Subsidies Increase Likelihood that Low-Income Mothers Will Work* (Washington, DC, December 1994).
45. Sandra L. Hofferth and Duncan Chaplin, *Childcare Quality vs. Availability: Do We Have to Trade One for the Other?* (Washington, DC: The Urban Institute Press, 1994), p. 2.
46. *Cost, Quality and Child Outcomes in Child Care Centers: Public Report* (University of Colorado at Denver, Center for Research on Economic and Social Policy, April 1995); *The State of America's Children Yearbook 1995* (Washington, DC: Children's Defense Fund, 1995), p. 40.
47. *The State of America's Children*, p. 40.
48. *The State of America's Children*, p. 43.
49. David van Biema, "The Storm over Orphanages," *Time*, 12/12/94, p. 58.
50. Charles Murray, "The Coming White Underclass," *WSJ*, 10/29/93, p. A14.
51. Furstenberg Jr. and Cherlin, *Divided Families*
52. Van Biema, p. 59.
53. Celia W. Dugger, "Displaced by the Welfare Wars," *NYT*, 2/26/95, p. D1.
54. Douglas J. Besharov, "Orphanages Aren't Welfare Reform," *NYT*, 12/20/94, p. A23.
55. Steven A. Holmes, "G.O.P. Seeks Shift in Child Welfare," *NYT*, 3/13/95, p. A7.
56. Elizabeth Shogren and Elizabeth Mehren, "Close Look Suggests Role of Orphanages a Complex One," *LAT*, 12/26/94, p. A1.

Robert Gumpert / Impact Visuals

MYTH "The first principle is that in order to move up, the poor must not only work, they must work harder than the classes above them. Every previous generation of the lower class has made such efforts. But the current poor, white even more than black, are refusing to work hard."[1]   —George Gilder, writer

REALITY

Many welfare recipients work hard.

- Since 1981, welfare policy has discouraged paid work by imposing a dollar-for-dollar reduction of benefits for money earned after only 3 months of work. Recipients also lost their health insurance through Medicaid after 1 year of employment. Nonetheless, many women who receive AFDC already work for pay.

- A study of over 1,000 women who received AFDC between 1984 and 1990 showed that over 40% engaged in a substantial amount of paid work, either combining work with welfare or cycling back and forth.[2]

- Intensive interviews with 50 welfare families in the Chicago area in 1988 and 1990 showed that about 20% worked under the table or off the books because they could not survive on welfare benefits alone.[3]

Child care costs make full-time wage earning uneconomical for many mothers.

- Working full-time, full-year at a minimum wage of $4.25 an hour, a single mother of 2 could earn $8,840 and be eligible for an Earned Income Tax Credit (EITC) of as much as $2,528 in 1994, for a total of $11,368. This is more than the estimated value of AFDC, Food Stamps, and Medicaid combined (about $9,000). However, unsubsidized child care expenses for 2 children (not to mention other work-related costs such as payroll taxes, clothing, and transportation) make up more than the difference. Many single mothers are worse off economically if they work for pay.[4]

- Mothers living in states with more generous AFDC benefits return to work more quickly than mothers living in states with less generous benefits, probably because they get more generous child care subsidies.[5]

Copyright, 1995, Boston Globe. Distributed by Los Angeles Times Syndicate. Reprinted with permission.

"I can tell you as a former welfare mother that the main reason families are on welfare in the first place is because there aren't enough jobs that pay a family wage, and there aren't the support systems like child care and health care so that they can get off welfare and go into the workforce."[6]

REP. LYNN WOOLSEY, D–California

MYTH "Almost two thirds of AFDC recipients will be on the welfare rolls for more than 8 years during their lifetime."[7]   —Republican Study Committee

"Current welfare programs have enslaved the poor."[8] —Rep. Bill Goodling, R–Pennsylvania

REALITY

Many welfare recipients are struggling to get off the rolls.

- About 40% of those who enter leave within 1 year; another 28% leave within 2 years.[9]

- In determining how long people stay on welfare, it is important to distinguish between those who are currently receiving assistance and those who have ever entered it. Imagine a 10-bed hospital in which 6 of the beds are occupied through the year by chronically ill patients who do not leave the hospital. The other 4 beds, though, are occupied by patients who stay just 1 month. At any one time, there are 10 people in the hospital; during the entire year, however, 54 spend time there [6 + (4 x 12)]. At any one time, 60% of those in the hospital are individuals who will be there the entire year; but only 6 out of the yearly total of 54 who pass through, or 11%, spend the entire year there.[10]

The real difficulty is not getting off welfare, but staying off. Many
women are forced to reapply because they are unable to find secure, adequately paid jobs that provide health insurance for themselves and their children.

- Roughly half of families who leave AFDC or Food Stamps find it necessary to return at a later date.[11]

- Between one-half and two-thirds of all women who leave welfare do so because they find a paying job. Relatively few of these jobs, however, are permanent.[12]

- A survey of women who participated in California's employment and training program for welfare recipients showed that 25% were laid off and 13% were fired. The remainder quit because of job-related problems, work-family conflicts, or interpersonal problems.[13]

A 5-year time limit on welfare without adequate guarantees of employment, child care, and health insurance is unrealistic.

- Total time spent on AFDC for those who ever receive it has averaged about 6 years.[14]

"Welfare is not a trap from which no one ever emerges. It sustains many families for a reasonable number of months after a death, divorce, or the birth of a child. It functions in place of unemployment insurance for some women. . . ."[15]

JANE KATZ, journalist

Scott Menchin

MYTH

"The trick, it seems clear, is to create incentives to draw more and more people up into the ranks of the middle class; once there, they'll try hard not to slide back."[16]
—Unsigned editorial, The Wall Street Journal

"The current welfare system, trying to give people material wealth and lift them out of poverty, is luring them into a kind of spiritual poverty by destroying their families and their incentives to work."[17]
—Rep. Jim McCrery, R-Louisiana

REALITY

Poor people don't need greater incentives to get out of poverty. Being poor is not fun.

- The real value of benefits on AFDC and Food Stamps combined has declined more than 20% since 1971.[18]

- The real value of the minimum wage was lower in 1995 than it was in 1950.

All forms of insurance, including welfare, or social insurance, create some disincentives. Car insurance may tempt drivers to be a bit careless about how they drive. Health insurance may tempt people to make an unnecessary doctor's appointment. Social Security may tempt people to save less and stop working at an earlier age. Unemployment insurance (including the privately negotiated "golden parachutes" that many top executives enjoy) may tempt people to get themselves fired. But the cost of such disincentives is small compared with the benefits that insurance provides.

The only incentives that conservatives advocate for the poor are those that save money for the rich. An alternative to the existing AFDC system would be to provide assistance to all poor families, whether or not a father is present in the home, and to provide the increased education, job training, and child care that would make it possible for mothers to find and keep decent jobs.[19] Creating such positive incentives would cost money. Instead, Congress has consistently chosen to cut taxes for the affluent.

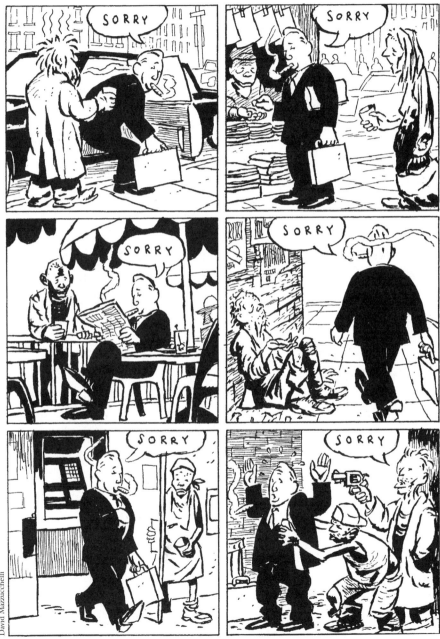

David Mazzucchelli

"To be sure, some individuals do abuse the welfare system . . . [but] such cases constitute a very small fraction of the overall welfare population. Most welfare recipients want a better life for themselves and their children; they don't enjoy being on government assistance; and they persevere in the face of countless hardships and handicaps. Ultimately, they cling to the American dream despite the formidable odds against them."[20]

MARK RANK, sociologist

MYTH

"It's bad for children to live with a parent who does nothing but hang around the house."[21]
—Governor William Weld of Massachusetts

"This raises the specter of a 'day care economy' in which women stay in their homes, not interacting with the labor market or picking up job skills."[22]
—Paul Offner, legislative aide to Sen. Daniel Patrick Moynihan, D—New York

REALITY

Taking care of children is a valuable, albeit underpaid, form of work.

- Children are public goods. All citizens have a claim on the earnings of the future generation, who will pay taxes to help pay off the federal budget deficit and support the Social Security system.

Just because work is unpaid doesn't mean that it is unproductive.

- In the nineteenth century, housewives and mothers were enumerated as members of the labor force by the census of Massachusetts, as well as the census of Great Britain.[23]

- Most economists now agree that nonmarket work, including child rearing, makes an important contribution to economic welfare. In Europe, many countries now estimate the value of nonmarket work and add it to their measure of total economic output.[24]

- Employed women, especially mothers, work much longer hours than men because they assume a disproportionate share of family care responsibilities. A 1992 survey of workers with children and employed spouses found that women spent about 61 hours doing paid and unpaid work every week, compared with about 46 hours spent by men.[25]

Parents need the flexibility to define their own balance between time devoted to paid work and to family work.

- In 1993, only about 28% of married women with children under 6 worked full-time for pay.[26] Many of these mothers benefited from the presence in the home of a father who was able to help with child care.

"In today's economy a woman is considered lazy when she's at home taking care of her children. And to me that's not laziness. If she's doing a good job at that, she has to use a lot of skills. And she's putting in more than forty hours a week when she's taking care of her family. And that's not laziness. Let some of these men that work in the government, let some of them stay home and do that. They'll find that a woman is not lazy when she's taking care of her family."[27]

DENISE TURNER, welfare recipient

MYTH

"If working steadily at any job is enough to avoid poverty in the great majority of cases, then features of the economy become largely irrelevant to poverty or dependency. Motivation is inevitably more at issue than opportunity."[28]
—Lawrence Mead, political scientist

REALITY

Working steadily at a job is *not* enough to avoid poverty.

- In 1994, an individual working full-time at the minimum wage earned $8,840 a year. The EITC could add as much as $2,528, for a total of $11,368. The poverty line for a family of 3 in that year was $11,817.[29]

Jim West / Impact Visuals

"Jobs—in abundance and
of good quality—are the
most needed and most per-
manent solution to the
poverty problem."[34]

BRADLEY SCHILLER,
economist

**The percentage of workers who
earn poverty-level wages and receive few
or no benefits has increased in recent years.**

- In 1993, 27% of all workers earned less than the amount needed to keep a family of 4 above the poverty level, compared with 24% in 1973.[30] Government programs intended to help workers displaced from their jobs, such as Unemployment Insurance, were cut back in the 1980s.[31]

**Women are more likely than men to earn
wages below the poverty level.**

- The hourly wage required for a full-time, full-year worker to bring a family of 3 to the poverty threshold and pay day-care costs for 1 child in 1991 was $6.67. Almost half of all women workers earned less than this mini-mum sufficiency wage in 1991.[32]

**If all current welfare
recipients found jobs, they
would either displace other
workers or reduce their wages.**

- Competition from former welfare recipients could cost low-wage earners about $36 billion, more than federal and state expenditures on AFDC in 1994.[33]

MYTH "Unfortunately, the federal government has never run a successful job training program. Even the much heralded Job Training Partnership Act produces graduates who earn the same as workers who don't participate in the JTPA program."[35]
—Republican Study Committee

REALITY

The United States has given up on job training.

- In 1993, the federal government spent only about $6.7 billion on employment and training programs, compared with about $18.2 billion in 1980 (in inflation-adjusted $1993).[36]

- Private-sector training offers little support. Only 4% of young workers without college degrees in the U.S. get any formal training at work, compared with over 70% for young people in Germany. In Japan, over one-third of all workers participated in workplace training within the past 2 years.[37]

With job training, you get what you pay for. Cheap programs don't provide good results.

- A recent study of the Job Training Partnership Act found that the benefits for persons receiving training outweighed the costs and successfully improved earnings for adult women participants. But modest expenditures produced only modest gains: 2 1/2 years later, women made only about $470 more a year than those who did not participate. Not surprisingly, this was not enough to significantly reduce receipt of AFDC or Food Stamps.[38]

Ricky Flores / Impact Visuals

Ricky Flores / Impact Visuals

A college diploma is the best ticket out of poverty.

PERCENTAGE OF WOMEN IN POVERTY BY DIFFERENT EDUCATIONAL LEVELS IN 1993 [39]

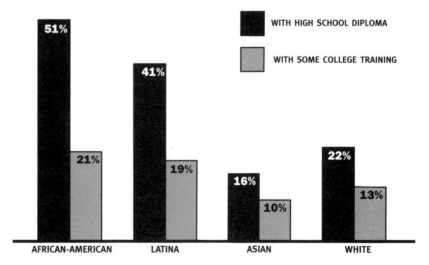

WITH HIGH SCHOOL DIPLOMA

WITH SOME COLLEGE TRAINING

AFRICAN-AMERICAN		LATINA		ASIAN		WHITE	
51%	21%	41%	19%	16%	10%	22%	13%

See p. 142 for abbreviations used in notes.

1. George Gilder, *Wealth and Poverty* (New York: Basic Books, 1981), p. 68.

2. Heidi I. Hartmann and Roberta Spalter-Roth, *The Real Employment Opportunities of Women Participating in AFDC: What the Market Can Provide* (Washington, DC: IWPR, October 23, 1993), p. 3.

3. Christopher Jencks, *Rethinking Social Policy: Race, Poverty, and the Underclass* (Cambridge: Harvard University Press, 1992), p. 208.

4. On the value of the EITC, see *1994 Green Book*, p. 700. On child care costs, see Sandra L. Hofferth and Duncan Chaplin, *Child Care Quality vs. Availability: Do We Have to Trade One for the Other?* (Washington, DC: The Urban Institute Press, 1994), p. 2. For another comparison of benefits with wages, see Jason DeParle, "When Giving Up Welfare for Job Just Doesn't Pay," *NYT*, 7/8/92, p. A1.

5. Sandra L. Hofferth and Duncan Chaplin, *Caring for Young Children While Parents Work: Public Policies and Private Strategies* (Washington, DC: The Urban Institute Press), 1994, p.4.

6. Quoted in Republican Study Committee, *Running from Reality: How Liberals Can't Accept the Failure of The Welfare State* (Washington, DC, 5/19/94), p. 5.

7. Republican Study Committee, p. 5.

8. Quoted in Robert Pear, "House Takes Up Legislation to Dismantle Social Programs," *NYT*, 3/22/95, p. A17.

9. Peter Gottschalk, Sara McLanahan, and Gary Sandefur, "Dynamics of Poverty and Welfare Participation," in *Confronting Poverty: Prescriptions for Change*, ed. Sheldon Danziger, Gary Sandefur, and Daniel Weinberg (Cambridge: Harvard University Press, 1994), p. 96; figures represent an average of those for black and nonblack recipients.

10. Inspired by a similar calculation by Teresa Amott, "The War on Welfare," *Dollars and Sense*, November–December 1993, p. 13.

11. Gottschalk, McLanahan, and Sandefur, p. 94.

12. LaDonna Pavetti, "Who Spends Longer Periods of Time Receiving Welfare?" in *Looking Before We Leap: Social Science and Welfare Reform*, ed. R. Kent Weaver and William T. Dickens (Washington, DC: The Brookings Institution, 1995), p. 40.

13. Pavetti, p. 40.

14. Gottschalk, McLanahan, and Sandefur, p.39.

15. Jane Katz, "Who's on Welfare?" *Federal Reserve Bank of Boston Regional Review* 5, no. 3 (Summer 1995), p. 20.

16. "Incentives," unsigned editorial, *WSJ*, 3/30/95, p. A14.

17. Pear, p. A1.

18. Carmen D. Solomon, *Aid to Families with Dependent Children (AFDC): Need Standards, Payment Standards, and Maximum Benefits*, Congressional Research Service, Report to Congress (Washington, DC, 1/18/95), p. 29.

19. See, for instance, Michael P. Keane, "A New Idea for Welfare Reform," *Federal Reserve Bank of Minneapolis Quarterly Review* 19, no. 2 (Spring 1995), pp. 2–28.

20. Mark Rank, *Living on the Edge: The Realities of Welfare in America* (New York: Columbia University Press, 1994), p. 5.

21. Ruth Conniff, "Bad Welfare," *The Progressive* 58, no. 9 (August 1994), p. 20.

22. Paul Offner, "Day Careless," *The New Republic*, 4/18/94, p. 19.

23. Nancy Folbre, "The Unproductive Housewife: Her Evolution in Nineteenth-Century Economic Thought," *Signs: Journal of Women in Culture and Society* 16, no. 3 (1991), pp. 463–84.

24. Nancy Folbre, "Domesticate the Gross Product," *Dollars and Sense*, March/April 1994, p. 7.

25. Ellen Galinsky, James T. Bond, and Dana Friedman, *The National Study of the Changing Workforce* (New York: Families and Work Institute, 1993), p. 47.

26. Calculated by Randy Albelda from the 1994 Current Population Survey computer tapes.

27. Quoted in Rank, p. 122.

28. Lawrence Mead, *The New Politics of Poverty: The Nonworking Poor in America* (New York: Basic Books, 1992), p. 212.

29. *1994 Green Book*, p. 700.

30. Lawrence Mishel and Jared Bernstein, *The State of Working America, 1994–95* (Armonk, NY: M.E. Sharpe, 1994), p. 126.

31. Center on Hunger, Poverty, and Nutrition, *Statement on Key Welfare Reform Issues: The Empirical Evidence* (Medford, MA: Tufts University, 1995), p. 14.

32. Heidi Hartmann and Roberta Spalter-Roth, *The Labor Market, the Working Poor, and Welfare Reform: Policy Suggestions for the Clinton Administration* (Washington DC: IWPR, December 9, 1992).

33. Economic Policy Institute, "EPI Report Finds Welfare Reform Will Cause Low-Wage Worker Wages to Fall by Nearly 12% Nationally," press release, 10/4/95, Washington, DC.

34. Bradley Schiller, *The Economics of Poverty and Discrimination* (Englewood Cliffs, NJ: Prentice-Hall, 1989), p. 210.

35. Republican Study Committee, p. 6.

36. *SA 1994*, pp. 334–35, Table 509.

37. Lisa Lynch, *Strategies for Workplace Training: Lessons from Abroad* (Washington, DC: Economic Policy Institute, 1993), p. 14.

38. Howard Bloom and others, *National Job Training Partnership Act Study* (Bethesda, MD: Abt Associates Inc., January 1994).

39. Calculated from 1994 Current Population Survey computer tapes; Latinos may be of any race.

The Economy

Earl Dotter / Impact Visuals

MYTH

"What happened in the 1980s—prosperity at home (the longest period of peacetime growth in this nation's history: fifty-nine consecutive growth months), strength abroad—directly contradicts every liberal shibboleth."[1]

—Rush Limbaugh

REALITY

Most families have experienced increased economic stress during the 1980s and 1990s.

- Both average hourly wages and median weekly earnings are lower now in terms of real purchasing power than they were in the 1970s.[2]

- Real wages have declined most dramatically for those without a college degree.

- Only those families who were able to send another person, usually a wife and mother, into paid employment have been able to increase their total income. They did so at the expense of time previously devoted to family labor, including child care.[3]

CHANGES IN REAL HOURLY WAGES, 1973–1993[4]

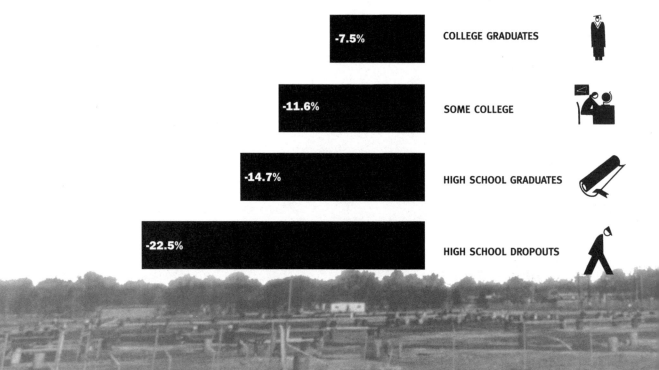

-7.5% COLLEGE GRADUATES

-11.6% SOME COLLEGE

-14.7% HIGH SCHOOL GRADUATES

-22.5% HIGH SCHOOL DROPOUTS

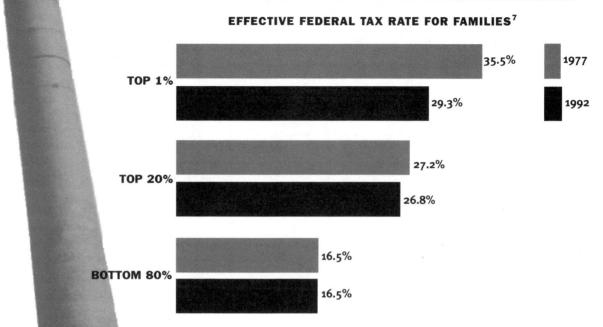

EFFECTIVE FEDERAL TAX RATE FOR FAMILIES[7]

TOP 1%
: 35.5% — 1977
: 29.3% — 1992

TOP 20%
: 27.2%
: 26.8%

BOTTOM 80%
: 16.5%
: 16.5%

The threat of job loss increased, even among older, better-educated, and highly paid workers.

Downsizing, layoffs, and general restructuring increased the likelihood of an unexpected decline in earnings, especially among lower-income workers.[5]

Many workers have lost access to job-related benefits.

- The percentage of full-time employees in medium-sized and large firms who enjoy fully employer-financed health care fell from 71% in 1980 to 37% in 1993.[6]

- The percentage of full-time employees in medium-sized and large firms eligible for retirement benefits fell from 87% to 78% over the same period.[8]

Only the richest Americans are paying lower taxes than they were in the 1970s (see graph).

- Increases in Social Security taxes have counterbalanced slight declines in the income tax.

Robert Fox/Impact Visuals

MYTH "The ability of the liberals to increase spending has outpaced anything Republicans could do in raising taxes."[9] —Newt Gingrich

REALITY

Tax breaks for the rich, not spending on the poor, caused today's federal budget deficit.

- Federal spending today is about the same as a percentage of what the country produces as it was in 1975 (see graph).

- The tax rate on the rich has declined at the expense of ordinary working people. Tax cuts implemented in 1978 and 1981 on the richest 1% lowered tax revenues. If 1977 tax rates had been in effect in 1992, the government would have enjoyed an additional $164 billion—$84 billion in additional direct revenues and $80 billion in reduced interest on debt accumulated as a result of tax cuts.[11]

- State and local taxes are more regressive than federal taxes; they take a bigger bite out of low incomes than out of high ones. No wonder affluent voters are generally in favor of decentralizing public spending.[12]

FEDERAL SPENDING AS A PERCENTAGE OF GROSS DOMESTIC PRODUCT[10]

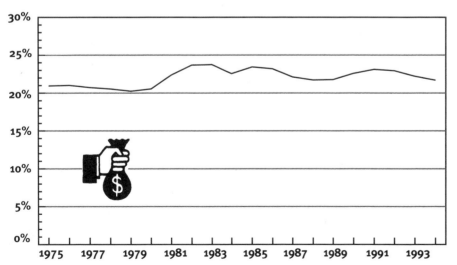

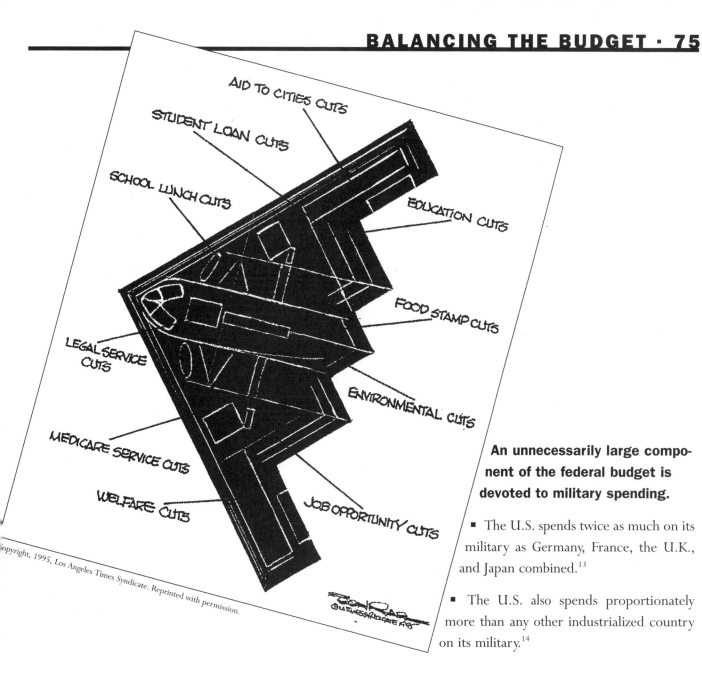

AID TO CITIES CUTS

STUDENT LOAN CUTS

SCHOOL LUNCH CUTS

EDUCATION CUTS

FOOD STAMP CUTS

LEGAL SERVICE CUTS

ENVIRONMENTAL CUTS

MEDICARE SERVICE CUTS

WELFARE CUTS

JOB OPPORTUNITY CUTS

Copyright, 1995, Los Angeles Times Syndicate. Reprinted with permission.

An unnecessarily large component of the federal budget is devoted to military spending.

- The U.S. spends twice as much on its military as Germany, France, the U.K., and Japan combined.[13]

- The U.S. also spends proportionately more than any other industrialized country on its military.[14]

MYTH "Did the rich get richer and the poor get poorer during the Reagan years? No, or at least not much, if at all."[15]
—John C. Weicher, senior fellow, Hudson Institute

REALITY

Inequality in wealth in the U.S. is at its worst point since the 1920s.

- The richest 20% of all households held nearly 85% of U.S. household wealth in 1989.[16]

- The rich are getting richer. The top 20% of wealth holders received 99% of the total gain in marketable wealth between 1983 and 1989. The top 1% alone garnered about 62%.[17]

- Wealth is now more unequally distributed in the U.S. than in other developed countries, including Great Britain.[18]

PERCENT OF TOTAL HOUSEHOLD WEALTH CONTROLLED BY THE TOP 1%[19]

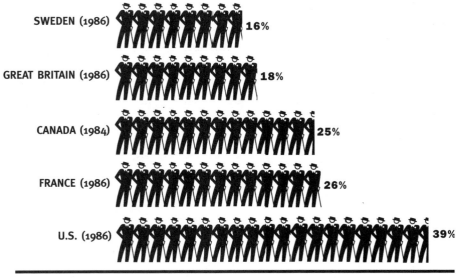

SWEDEN (1986) 16%

GREAT BRITAIN (1986) 18%

CANADA (1984) 25%

FRANCE (1986) 26%

U.S. (1986) 39%

Peter Kuper

Income inequality has also increased.

- Call it the comfortable class. Households with a money income greater than $60,500 were in the top 20% of the income distribution in 1993. This group has steadily improved its standard of living relative to those in the bottom 20%. In 1992, it received about 11 times as much, compared with only 7.5 times as much in 1969.[20]

- The top 5% of income earners have really made out. In 1992, they claimed more than 18% of all household income.[21]

"Economic segregation in this country is so rigid that we literally don't know one another anymore."[22]

MOLLY IVINS

MYTH

"If you create incentives, and in fact demand work, I think you'll see people move into the work force."[23]
—Governor George Pataki, New York

REALITY

Many people who want to work can't find jobs.

- Unemployment rates have been drifting upward over time. They averaged about 4.4% in the 1950s, 6.2% in the 1970s, and 6.5% in 1990–1994.[24]

- Public policy in this country seeks to maintain an unemployment rate of over 5%. When unemployment rates dip below that figure, the Federal Reserve Bank begins worrying about inflation and increases interest rates. This reduces the level of economic activity and sends unemployment back up.

Unemployment rates are particularly high among African-Americans, Latinos, and youths of all races and ethnicities.

- In some poor urban neighborhoods, such as New York's Harlem, the official unemployment rate is about 18%. There is fierce competition for inner-city fast-food jobs, where the ratio of job applicants to hires is about 14 to 1.[25]

Many welfare recipients are particularly ill equipped to compete in the labor market.

- Fewer than 55% of AFDC mothers have completed high school. Only about 1% have graduated from college.[26]

- Studies of what happened when Pennsylvania, Ohio, and Michigan eliminated their General Assistance programs show that most former recipients were unable to get and keep jobs.[27]

AVERAGE UNEMPLOYMENT RATE, BY RACE, ETHNICITY, AND AGE IN 1994[28]

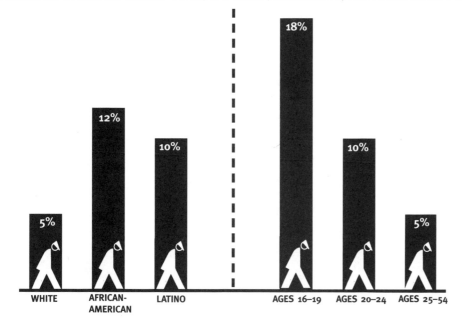

WHITE	AFRICAN-AMERICAN	LATINO	AGES 16–19	AGES 20–24	AGES 25–54
5%	12%	10%	18%	10%	5%

What this boils down to is that AFDC recipients, particularly those on the Federal rolls for some time, will join the back of a very long unemployment line."[29]

KATHERINE NEWMAN,
anthropologist

MYTH "The minimum wage turns out to be one of our leading killers—a killer of economic growth and opportunity among the young, the poor, and the minority community. It's time to stop it before it kills again."[30]
—Pete Du Pont, heir to the Du Pont family fortune

REALITY

A modest hike in the minimum wage would not increase unemployment.

- Studies of what actually happened when minimum wages were increased at the federal level and in the state of New Jersey show no increase in unemployment, even among teens.[31] Some fast-food businesses that paid the minimum found that they were able to fill more jobs with higher wages.

- Over 100 well-known economists, including 3 Nobel Prize winners, have signed a statement backing a $0.90 hike in the minimum wage over 2 years.[32]

The current minimum wage is completely inadequate.

- At $4.25 an hour, full-time, year-round minimum wage earners get $8,840 a year. Even with the maximum Earned Income Tax Credit of $2,528 in 1994, this is not enough for a worker with 2 dependents to escape poverty.[33]

- The minimum wage is worth less now than it was in 1950. Inflation has increased more rapidly than hikes in the minimum; $1.25 could buy more in 1950 than $4.25 could in 1995.

- Few minimum-wage jobs provide any health or retirement benefits.

OVER 10 MILLION EXPLOITED

PAYROLL

Paul Corio

Many different kinds of people earn the minimum wage.

- In 1994, 43% of minimum-wage earners worked full-time, and 39% were the sole earners in their family. Only 15% were teens; 64% were women.[34]

An increase in the minimum wage would have a ripple effect, improving the bargaining power of all low-paid workers.

MYTH

"Dependence passes between generations; children raised in families that receive welfare assistance are themselves three times more likely to be on welfare than other children when they become adults."[35]
—The Heritage Foundation

REALITY

Poverty, not welfare, gets transmitted from generation to generation.

- Women who grow up on welfare are more likely to receive welfare than other women. But this doesn't mean that welfare causes intergenerational dependence. Children who grow up in poor families are more likely than others to be poor, just as children who grow up in rich families are more likely than others to be rich.[36]

- About 25% of all daughters of AFDC recipients receive AFDC in adulthood.[37]

- Few, if any, studies have closely examined the influence of family income on daughters' future earnings, but adult sons have a 60% chance of having approximately the same income as their fathers.[38]

A family's income level is a good predictor of how well its children will be educated.

- Public school quality, largely determined by educational expenditures per student, is strongly influenced by the size of the local tax base. Wealthy communities generally have better schools than poor ones.

- School quality has a positive effect on future earnings, even controlling for differences in family background.[39]

- In 1992, more than 40% of high school dropouts explained that they had to support their families, had to care for a family member, or were unable to work and go to school at the same time.[40]

Poor people have less wealth to transfer to their children.

- In 1989, more than half the poor had no financial assets at all, and more than half the remainder had less than $1,000.[41]

- AFDC recipients lose eligibility if they accumulate savings of more than about $1,000.

"The real explanation of why the poor are where they are is that they made the mistake of being born to the wrong parents, in the wrong section of the country, in the wrong industry, or in the wrong racial or ethnic group. Once that mistake has been made, they could have been paragons of will and morality, but most of them would never even have had a chance to get out of the other America."[42]

MICHAEL HARRINGTON, writer

Scott Cunningham

See p. 142 for abbreviations used in notes.

1. Rush Limbaugh, *See, I Told You So* (New York: Pocket Books, 1993), p. 121.
2. Nancy Folbre and the CPE, *The New Field Guide to the U.S. Economy* (New York: The New Press, 1995), pp. 2.5–2.6.
3. Folbre, p. 6.1.
4. Lawrence Mishel and Jared Bernstein, The Economic Policy Institute, *The State of Working America 1994-95* (Armonk, NY: M.E. Sharpe, 1994), p. 140, Table 3.18.
5. Gene Koretz, "Why Incomes Grew Less Equal," *Business Week*, 4/20/95, p. 24.
6. BLS press release, 9/30/94, Tables 3 and 5.
7. Wallace C. Peterson, *Silent Depression: The Fate of the American Dream* (New York: W.W. Norton, 1994), p. 105. See also Citizens for Tax Justice, *Inequality and the Federal Budget Deficit* (Washington, DC, 1991).
8. BLS, Tables 3 and 5.
9. Newt Gingrich, *To Renew America* (New York: HarperCollins, 1995), p. 89.
10. *Economic Report of the President 1995* (Washington, DC: GPO, 1995), p. 274, Table B1; p. 367, Table B79.
11. Citizens for Tax Justice, *Inequality and the Federal Budget Deficit* (Washington, DC, 1991), p. 8.
12. Folbre, p. 5.14.
13. Folbre, p. 5.9.
14. *SA 1994*, p. 885, Table 1409; p. 864, Table 1370.
15. John C. Weicher, "Getting Richer (At Different Rates)," *WSJ*, 6/14/95, p. A18.
16. Steven Sass, "Passing the Buck," *Federal Reserve Bank of Boston, Regional Review* 5, no. 3 (Summer 1995), p. 16.
17. Edward N. Wolff, "How the Pie Is Sliced: America's Growing Concentration of Wealth," *The American Prospect*, Summer 1995, p 58.
18. Wolff, p. 59.
19. Same as above.
20. *Income, Poverty, and Valuation of Noncash Benefits: 1993* (CPR, P-60, no. 188), p. 40, Table 10. "For Richer, for Poorer," *The Economist*, 11/5/94, p. 19.
21. *Money Income of Households, Families, and Persons in the U.S. 1992* (CPR, P-60, no. 184), pp. B6-7, Table B-3.
22. Molly Ivins, "Yafers in Lockstep," *The Texas Observer*, 4/21/95, p. 13.
23. Quoted in Katherine S. Newman, "What Inner-City Jobs for Welfare Moms?" *NYT*, 5/20/95, p. 23.
24. *Economic Report of the President 1994* (Washington, DC: GPO, 1994), p. 314, Table B-40.
25. Newman, p. 23.
26. Gary Burtless, "What Is the Proper Balance Among Various Types of Welfare-to-Work Programs," in *Looking Before We Leap: Social Science and Welfare Reform*, ed. R. Kent Weaver and William T. Dickens (Washington, DC: The Brookings Institution, 1995), p. 54.
27. Center on Social Welfare Policy and Law, *Jobless, Penniless, Often Homeless: State General Assistance Cuts Leave "Employables" Struggling for Survival*, Publication 80, New York, February 1994.
28. BLS, *Employment and Earnings* 41, no. 10 (October 1994): p. 18, Table A-9; p. 19, Table A-10.
29. Newman, p. 23.
30. Pete Du Pont, "Pay Hazard," *National Review*, May 1, 1995, p. 74.
31. David Card and Alan Krueger, *Myth and Measurement: The New Economics of the Minimum Wage* (Princeton: Princeton University Press, 1995); Lawrence Mishel, Jared Bernstein, and Edith Rasell, "Who Wins with a Higher Minimum Wage," Economic Policy Institute Briefing Paper (Washington, DC, February, 1995); John McDermott, "Bare Minimum: A Too-Low Minimum Wage Keeps All Wages Down," *Dollars and Sense*, July–August 1995, pp. 26–29.
32. Center on Budget and Policy Priorities, "Leading Economists Call for Higher Minimum Wage," press release, October 2, 1995, Washington, DC.
33. U.S. Department of Labor, "Making Work Pay: The Case for Raising the Minimum Wage," press release, February 1995.
34. Same as above.
35. Heritage Foundation, *Combatting Family Disintegration, Crime, and Dependence: Welfare Reform and Beyond* (Washington, DC, 4/8/94), p. 8.
36. Leonard Beeghley, *The Structure of Social Stratification in the United States* (Boston: Allyn and Bacon, 1989); Gary Solon, "Intergenerational Income Mobility in the United States," *American Economic Review* 82, no. 3 (June 1992), pp. 393–408.
37. Peter Gottschalk, Sara McLanahan, and Gary D. Sandefur, "Dynamics of Poverty and Welfare Participation" in *Confronting Poverty: Prescriptions for Change*, ed. Sheldon Dannziger, Gary D. Sandefur, and Daniel H. Weinberg, (Cambridge: Harvard University Press, 1994), p. 1062.
38. Jere Behrman and Paul Taubman, "The Intergenerational Correlation Between Children's Adult Earnings and Their Parents' Income: Results from the Michigan Panel Study of Dynamics," *Review of Income and Wealth* 36, no. 2 (June 1990), pp. 115–27.
39. David Card and Alan Kreuger, "Does School Quality Matter? Returns to Education and the Characteristics of Public Schools in the United States," *Journal of Political Economy* 100, no. 1 (February 1992), p. 1040.
40. *Drop-Out Rates in the United States 1992*, National Center for Education Statistics.
41. Patricia Ruggles, *Drawing the Line: Alternative Poverty Measures and Their Implications for Public Policy* (Washington, DC: The Urban Institute Press, 1990), p. 150.
42. Michael Harrington, *The Other America: Poverty in the United States* (Baltimore, MD: Penguin, 1963), p. 182.

Sex, Lies,
and Righteous
Indignation

MYTH

"In a reversal of the usual pattern in civilized societies, the women have the income and the ties to government authority and support. The men are economically and socially subordinate."[1]
—George Gilder, writer

"The man is no longer essential for financial support. Welfare is given with good intentions, but it has emasculated John Q. Stud. He has reverted to irresponsibility."[2]
—Rush Limbaugh

REALITY

Men still earn far more income and experience far less poverty than women.

- In the first half of 1995, women working full-time, year-round earned $0.76 cents for every $1.00 men earned.[3]

- In 1993, 15% of all women age 18 and over had incomes under the poverty line, compared with 10% of men in the same age group.[4]

The welfare state didn't cause family desertion. It was devised to deal with problems created by desertion.

- Economic development and the growth of a market economy began weakening family ties more than a century ago. In the early 1900s, many states passed laws requiring that adult children support indigent parents but found them difficult to enforce.[5] The problems of mothers raising children on their own began getting a great deal of attention about the same time. Though rates of divorce and out-of-wedlock births were low, marital desertion was not.[6]

- Not until 1975 did the U.S. government take any significant action to monitor or enforce paternal child support responsibilities.

Entrance into paid employment, not the welfare state, increases women's economic independence.

- Women make up more than 45% of the nation's paid labor force. About 60% of all women (compared with 75% of men) work for pay.[7]

- Women earn about as much as their husbands in nearly half of American households in which both spouses work for pay. Most husbands feel more grateful than threatened.[8]

"WELFARE'S LIKE A TRAFFIC ACCIDENT. IT CAN HAPPEN TO ANYBODY, BUT ESPECIALLY IT HAPPENS TO WOMEN. AND THAT IS WHY WELFARE IS A WOMEN'S ISSUE."[9]
— Johnnie Tillmon
WELFARE RIGHTS ACTIVIST

MYTH "Every night on the local news, you and I watch the welfare state undermining our society. The vast majority of Americans (96 percent by one recent poll) is ready to admit that the welfare state has failed."[10] —Newt Gingrich

REALITY

Most Americans want welfare reform that will genuinely help the poor, not just punish them.

- A majority of individuals polled in 1995 favored work requirements, but a majority also favored job training and subsidized child care. Fewer than half believed that unmarried women under age 18 should be ineligible.[11]

- Despite all the poor-bashing that has taken place in Congress and the media, more than half of all people surveyed in a *New York Times*/CBS News poll in late 1994 agreed that poverty was either wholly or partly due to circumstances beyond poor people's control.

- Most people did not agree that there should be any lifetime limit to benefits for the poor; 71% agreed that assistance should be available for recipients as long as they are working, and about 80% rejected the notion that foster care or orphanages should be used as a way of providing support to children while denying it to their mothers.[12]

Many people have been misinformed about existing programs and work requirements.

- Few people know that both AFDC and the Food Stamps program already impose work requirements.

- Most believe that the amount of money spent on programs for the poor is far greater than it really is. A poll of voters in 1994 found that 1 out of 5 mistakenly believed that welfare spending exceeded military spending and was the government's biggest expense.[13]

Poll results are very sensitive to the way questions are worded.

- In 1992, one poll showed that 44% of all respondents said we were spending too much on "welfare," but only 13% said we were spending too much on "assistance to the poor."[14]

- In 1994, asked if government spending on "welfare" should be increased, decreased, or kept about the same, 48% of all respondents said it should be decreased. But when asked if government spending on "poor children" should be increased, decreased, or kept about the same, only 9% said it should be decreased, and 47% said it should be increased.[15] About two-thirds of all beneficiaries of AFDC are children.

The "RALL" cartoon by Ted Rall is reprinted by permission of Chronicle features, San Francisco, CA.

"We already have very little self-esteem, so the last thing we need is to have the country turn around and point the finger at us and say we're the problem, but suddenly we're responsible for everything from the schools to the deficit. It's like ethnic cleansing. That's what it feels like."[16]

CAROL GAGNON, AFDC recipient

MYTH

"The intrusion of the state into charity killed the [charitable] impulse."[17]
—Donald McCloskey, economist

"Churches, synagogues and faith-based charities are the great untapped resource in the welfare reform debate."[18]
—Rep. Tim Hutchinson, R-Arkansas

REALITY

Private charity has never been sufficient to solve problems of poverty and unemployment. That is exactly why governments developed public assistance programs. In the original 13 colonies, towns provided food, housing, and occasionally, cash for their poor.

There is no evidence that welfare spending discourages charitable contributions. In fact, attacks on the "lifestyles" and "morality" of the poor probably discourage private as well as public contributions.

Charitable giving has declined along with average benefits to families on welfare.

- A study commissioned by the Independent Sector, a coalition of 800 voluntary organizations, shows that charitable giving by U.S. households declined by 24% between 1989 and 1993.[19]

- Very rich people are especially less likely to donate money to charity than they used to be. In 1979, individuals making more than $1 million (in inflation-adjusted dollars) gave more than 7% of their after-tax income to charity; by 1991, the figure had declined to less than 4%.[20] One probable reason was cuts in tax rates for the very rich, which made tax-deductible contributions less attractive to them.

Most charity does not go to the poor. In 1992, about $124 billion was spent on private philanthropy. But less than 10% was spent in the area of "human service."[21] Many contributions go to support churches, schools, and other nonprofit institutions that primarily serve the affluent, not to mention contributions to right-wing think tanks like the Heritage Foundation.[22]

Charities are already doing the best they can.

- Charity organizations, as well as many religious leaders, have publicly explained that they will not be able to compensate for cuts in government social welfare programs.[23]

- In fact, many charities will be forced to reduce spending because they get about 30% of their funding from government.[24]

"There are not enough social workers, not enough nuns, not enough Salvation Army workers to care for children who would be purged from the welfare rolls if a two-year limit were imposed."[25]

SEN. DANIEL PATRICK MOYNIHAN, D–New York

James Victore

MYTH

"The Chicago welfare queen has eighty names, thirty addresses, twelve social security cards and is collecting veteran's benefits on four nonexisting deceased husbands. . . . Her tax-free cash income alone is over $150,000."[26]

—Ronald Reagan, President

"Some people take advantage of the current welfare program's lax bureaucracy and simply live off welfare—generation after generation—by skillfully gaming the system."[27]

—Rep. Marge Roukema, R-New Jersey

Most Food Stamp fraud is carried out by vendors, not welfare recipients.

- Store owners in poor neighborhoods often illegally redeem Food Stamps for an amount in cash far below their face value and pocket the difference. Lax supervision and regulation have

REALITY

The extent of welfare fraud has been exaggerated.

- When reporters tracked down Ronald Reagan's "welfare queen," they discovered that the actual offender used 2 aliases to collect 23 public aid checks totaling $8,000.[28]

- New York City officials recently began fingerprinting welfare recipients to root out fraud but found very few duplicate claims, less than 1% of the total.[29]

- In order to supplement below-poverty level benefits, some AFDC recipients work "under the table" and do not report their earnings. They do this because under current rules, they are likely to lose their eligibility for benefits, including health care, even if their earnings fall well below the poverty line.[30]

resulted in many stores being approved to accept Food Stamps, even though they shouldn't be eligible because they don't sell groceries. According to a 1995 study, stores of questionable eligibility redeemed more than $42 million in Food Stamps between April 1994 and May 1995.[31]

Losses from tax evasion and white-collar crime are far more serious than welfare abuse.

- In 1993, the federal government lost about $150 billion

from tax evasion and inaccurate reporting, an amount greater than total federal and state spending on AFDC for the last 5 years. Despite these huge revenue losses, fewer than 1% of all individual tax returns were audited in 1992.[32]

- According to the Resolution Trust Corporation, which was set up to salvage failed savings and loans associations, about 81% of the more than $300 billion cost of the bailout was due to fraud or wrongdoing.[33]

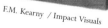
F.M. Kearny / Impact Visuals

"There are a lot of other lies that male society tells about welfare mothers: that AFDC mothers are immoral, that AFDC mothers are lazy, misuse their welfare checks, spend it all on booze and are stupid and incompetent. If people are willing to believe these lies, it's partly because they're just special versions of the lies that society tells about all women."[34]

JOHNNIE TILLMON,
welfare rights activist

MYTH "I'm just one voice in a virtual cacophony of media ultra-liberalism, but look at the result."[35] —Rush Limbaugh

REALITY

Most media coverage of welfare issues is conservative and male-dominated.

- The group Fairness and Accuracy in Reporting recently surveyed 6 of the most influential news outlets in the country. They found "a truncated spectrum of political opinion that favored conventional wisdom over dissent, a selection of policy experts that rarely stretched the debate, and a number of old myths persistently rehashed."[36]

Conservatives have built a large right-wing think tank and media machine.

- Between 1990 and 1993, grants to top right-wing magazines were more than 10 times greater than those to top left-wing magazines.[37]

The Heritage Foundation alone has had an enormous impact, especially on the welfare reform debate.

- In the first 100 days of the 1995 Congress, Heritage Foundation staff members testified before lawmakers 40 times.[38]

- With a budget of over $25 million and a staff of 150, it is the wealthiest think tank in Washington, D.C.[39]

- Only 40% of its budget goes to research; the rest goes to administration, marketing, and power lunches. According to the *Wall Street Journal*, the Heritage Foundation "more than other think tanks, has extended its political influence by spending more money on raising funds and promoting its thoughts than on researching them."[40]

"LIBERALS ALL OVER THE PLACE!"

Robert Grossman

MYTH

"By blaming everything on 'society,' contemporary liberals are really trying to escape the personal responsibility that comes with being an American. If 'society' is responsible for everything, then no one is personally responsible for anything."[41]

—Newt Gingrich

"Theirs is an anti-American credo, which abhors American political and governmental institutions and this nation's capitalistic economy. Their value system is at war with the Judeo-Christian tradition upon which this country was founded. . . ."[42]

—Rush Limbaugh

REALITY

Personal responsibility should be accompanied by social responsibility.

Liberals and other defenders of public assistance to the poor don't blame everything on society. We just don't blame everything on individuals. Sometimes people are doing the best they can. Why blame someone for not working if he or she genuinely can't find a job or if taking a job would put his or her children at risk?

America is supposed to be the Land of Opportunity.

Children who have an equal opportunity to compete are likely to become good competitors. But many children growing up in poverty lack the basic resources they need to get a good education and find a good job.

Social responsibility is central to the Jewish and Christian traditions.

"Woe to them that take away the right of the poor."
—Isaiah 10:1

"Defend the poor and fatherless; do justice to the afflicted and needy."
—Psalms 82:3

"Charity suffereth long, and is kind; charity envieth not; charity vaunteth not itself, is not puffed up, doth not behave itself unseemly, seeketh not her own, is not easily provoked, thinketh no evil."
—Corinthians 13:4–5

"Love thy neighbor as thyself."
—Matthew 5:43

H.L. Delgado / Impact Visuals

"All too many of those who live in affluent America ignore those who exist in poor America; in doing so, the affluent Americans will eventually have to face themselves with the question that Eichmann chose to ignore: How responsible am I for the well-being of my fellows? To ignore evil is to become an accomplice to it."[43]

MARTIN LUTHER KING JR., civil rights activist

See p. 142 for abbreviations used in notes.

1. George Gilder, "End Welfare Reform as We Know It," *The American Spectator*, June 1995, p. 24.
2. Rush Limbaugh, *The Way Things Ought to Be* (New York: Pocket Books, 1992), p. 196.
3. BLS, *Employment and Earnings* 42, no. 7 (July 1995), p. 154.
4. *Income, Poverty, and Valuation of Noncash Benefits: 1993* (CPR, P-60, 188): p. 22, Table 8.
5. See Nancy Folbre, *Who Pays for the Kids? Gender and the Structures of Constraint* (New York: Routledge, 1994).
6. Linda Gordon, *Pitied but Not Entitled: Single Mothers and the History of Welfare, 1890–1935* (New York: The Free Press, 1994).
7. *SA 1994*, p. 395, Table 615.
8. Michele Ingrassia and Pat Wingert, "The New Providers," *Newsweek*, 5/22/95, pp. 36–38.
9. Quoted in Teresa Amott, "Black Women and AFDC: Making Entitlement Out of Necessity," in *Women, Welfare, and the State*, ed. Linda Gordon (Madison: University of Wisconsin Press, 1990), p. 289.
10. Newt Gingrich, *To Renew America* (New York: HarperCollins, 1995), p. 9.
11. Joe Davidson, "Welfare Mothers Stress Importance of Building Self-Esteem If Aid System Is to Be Restructured," *WSJ*, 5/12/95, p. A14.
12. Maureen Dowd, "Americans Like G.O.P. Agenda but Split on How to Reach Goals," *NYT*, 12/15/94, p. A1.
13. Dowd, p. A1.
14. Robin Toner, "Politics of Welfare: Focusing on the Problems," *NYT*, 7/5/92, p. A1.
15. Holly Sklar, *Chaos or Community*, (Boston: South End Press), p. 73.
16. Quoted in Melinda Henneberger, "Welfare Bashing Finds Its Mark," *NYT*, 3/5/95, p. E5.
17. Donald McCloskey, "Bourgeois Virtue," *The American Scholar*, Spring 1994, p. 187.
18. Laurie Goodstein,"Churches May Not Be Able to Patch Budget Cuts," *WP*, 2/22/95, p. A1.
19. Goodstein, p. A1. See also Karl Vick, "Poll Shows Charitable Giving, Volunteering Still on Decline," *WP*, 10/19/94, p. A24.
20. Felicity Barringer, "Data Shows Fall in Giving by Rich Even as Ranks of Millionaires Grow," *NYT*, 5/24/92, p. 16.

21. *SA 1994*, p. 389, Table 610.
22. Teresa Odendahl, *Charity Begins at Home: Generosity and Self-Interest Among the Philanthropic Elite* (New York: Basic Books, 1990).
23. Goodstein, p. A1.
24. Joseph P. Shapiro and Jennifer Seter, "The Myths of Charity," *USNWR*, 1/16/95, p. 40.
25. Quoted in George F. Will, "Reformers Would Compound the Tragedy of Welfare," *BG*, 9/15/95, p. 31.
26. Quoted in Lou Cannon, *President Reagan: The Role of a Lifetime* (New York: Simon & Schuster, 1991), p. 518.
27. Quoted in "Welfare Reform, Current Programs, Financial Projections, Bill Summary," *Congressional Digest*, June-July 1995, p. 184.
28. Cannon, p. 518.
29. Kimberly J. McLarin, "Welfare Fingerprinting Finds Most People Are Telling Truth," *NYT*, 9/29/95, p. B1.
30. Christopher Jencks, *Rethinking Social Policy: Race, Poverty, and the Underclass* (Cambridge: Harvard University Press, 1992), p. 208.
31. Jennifer Dixon, "Lax Oversight Is Faulted in Food Stamp Trafficking," *BG*, 8/2/95.
32. *Reality on File* 53, no. 2770 (December 31, 1993), p. 973.
33. Gretchen Morgenson, "What Did Pop Expect to Happen When He Gave the Kid His Credit Card," *Forbes*, 9/28/92, pp. 97–98.
34. Quoted in Amott, p. 289.
35. Rush Limbaugh, *See, I Told You So* (New York: Pocket Books, 1993), p. 99.
36. Laura Flanders and Janine Jackson, "Public Enemy No. 1? Media's Welfare Debate Is a War on Poor Women," *Extra*, May/June 1995, p. 14.
37. Beth Schulman, "Foundations for a Movement: How the Right Wing Subsidizes Its Press," *Extra*, March/April 1995, p. 11.
38. Christopher Georges, "Conservative Heritage Foundation Finds Recipe for Influence: Ideas and Marketing = Clout," *WSJ*, 8/10/95, p. A10.
39. James Allen Smith, *The Idea Brokers: Think Tanks and the Rise of the New Policy Elite* (New York: The Free Press, 1991) p. 287; Georges, p. A10.
40. Georges, p. A10.
41. Gingrich, p. 39.
42. Limbaugh, p. 261.

43. Quoted in *America's New War on Poverty*, ed. Robert Lavelle and the Staff of Blackside (San Francisco: KQED Books, 1995), p. 184.

Overview

Corbis-Berrmann

Before 1862: Public assistance to poor provided on local level.

1862: Federal pensions provided for injured Union army Civil War veterans and/or their dependent survivors.

1890: Federal pensions extended to all Union army Civil War veterans and their dependents.

1897: Destitute Mothers Bill considered but rejected by New York State legislature.

1909: White House Conference on Children declares poor children should not be separated from their parents.

1911: First mothers' aid program established by a state.

1915: First old-age pension program established by a state.

1920: By this date, 40 states have mothers' aid laws, and 6 have old-age pensions.

1921: Federal Sheppard-Towner Act funds programs for maternal and child health; considered the first federal welfare program.

1929: Sheppard-Towner Act repealed.

"Bread for the needy, clothing for the naked, and houses for the homeless."[2]

CHANT OF 20,000 UNEMPLOYED PROTESTERS IN CHICAGO, 1873

Seth Tobocman & Barbara Lee

The U.S. has had a "welfare state" from the very beginning of its existence. Assistance was traditionally provided at the local level through town government. In the nineteenth century, more punitive policies were applied, such as confining all the poor, including orphans, to workhouses. This system did not prove satisfactory, even when public assistance was complemented by the growth of private philanthropic organizations.

Growing industrialization and the decline of family farming in many areas drew more and more people into wage employment that provided little economic security for elders or families lacking a male breadwinner. Many individuals found themselves without either family or farm to rely on in old age. Those who had served in the Union army during the Civil War were eligible for a generous federal pension. Still, by 1900, the elderly made up an alarming share of the almshouse population.

The economic problems of mothers on their own also intensified. Once considered economic assets, children became increasingly costly as educational requirements increased and opportunities for child labor declined. Fathers had once insisted on child custody in the event of divorce; but by the early 1900s, many were eager to avoid economic responsibility. Though divorce was rare, desertion was not, and policy makers began to worry about fatherless families in general. In 1900, nearly 10% of children lived with lone mothers, virtually the same proportion as in 1960.

Many reformers began to criticize the traditional system of close moral supervision of the poor in almshouses, particularly the placement of poor children in orphanages. Moreover, funding these institutions proved far more costly than assisting families in their own homes. In 1909, even conservative philanthropic groups such as the Charity Organization Societies agreed that poor children should not be separated from their parents. States began to enact pension programs for the elderly and mothers on their own, emphasizing that they represented public support and appreciation for recipients' contributions to society, not charity.

In 1921, the federal government approved the Sheppard-Towner Act, which provided support for maternity and child health programs. In just a few years, this legislation significantly reduced maternal and

"Private beneficence is totally inadequate to deal with the vast number of the city's disinherited."[4]

JANE ADDAMS, 1910

Seth Tobocman & Barbara Lee

"Poverty and suffering are increased and even caused by the relief intended to cure them . . . due to the moral effects of such relief."[3]

JOSEPHINE SHAW LOWELL, 1884

Knickerbocker

infant mortality. But the 1920s, rather like the early 1990s, witnessed a backlash against public assistance programs. In 1929, the Sheppard-Towner Act was repealed, largely because of heavy lobbying by the American Medical Association, which believed that government-sponsored health care would interfere with doctors' control. In that same year, however, a large stock market crash inaugurated the Great Depression, and a new period in U.S. economic and political history began.

1933: Federal Emergency Relief Act passed to meet the needs of the unemployed and the poor.

1935: Social Security Act sets up old-age insurance and assistance and unemployment insurance for covered workers (agricultural and domestic laborers excluded) and provided Aid for Dependent Children (ADC) for fatherless families, with strict restrictions on eligibility and no additional funding for adult caregivers.

1939: Survivors' benefits provided directly to widows and children through Social Security.

1945–1949: Veterans of World War II gain important benefits for life, including home mortgage subsidies, health care, and support for education through the GI Bill.

1952–1956: Social Security coverage extended to a wider range of employees. ADC adds support for primary caregiver and becomes Aid to Families with Dependent Children (AFDC).

1964: Equal Opportunity Act provides funds for job training and community action. Food Stamps program created.

1965: Medicare program establishes medical insurance for the elderly population. Medicaid program establishes assistance for some families living in poverty, especially the elderly in need of nursing home care.

1967: Work Incentive program (WIN) allows welfare recipients to keep some of their earnings and requires mothers to participate in job training if child care is available.

"No one has starved."[6]
HERBERT HOOVER,
assessing the seriousness of the
Great Depression in 1931

Knickerbocker

The Great Depression of 1929 worsened the plight of those who were already poor and pushed many people into a sudden poverty for which they could not be easily blamed. The urgent need for public assistance helped motivate the election of Franklin D. Roosevelt and the development of new relief programs, as well as the Social Security Act of 1935.

Social Security was funded with a payroll tax in order to make it appear similar to a pension system; in fact, most retirees and other beneficiaries gained benefits far greater than their actual contributions. In general, programs that provided benefits regardless of income levels, such as Social Security and veterans' benefits, expanded far more than assistance to the poor in the 1940s and 1950s.

Expenditures on AFDC were kept low by a variety of unconstitutional restrictions on individual behavior, such as the "no man in the house" rule. The welfare rights movement of the 1960s successfully contested these rules, and the political activism of the civil rights movement demanded an increase in economic opportunity. Lyndon Johnson officially declared war on poverty in 1964.

From the very beginning, however, it was a halfhearted fight. Increases in direct assistance to the poor remained small compared with Medicare, Medicaid, and boosts in Social Security retirement benefits, which helped a much larger percentage of the population, primarily the nonpoor. Legislators worried that AFDC was discouraging mothers from participating in the labor force and implemented the Work Incentive program in 1967. However, they did not provide sufficient funding—or child care—to help many mothers make the transition to paying jobs.

"I see one third of a nation ill-housed, ill-clad, ill-nourished."[7]
FRANKLIN D. ROOSEVELT, second inaugural address, 1937

"For the first time in America's history, poverty is on the run."[8]
LYNDON JOHNSON, 1964

Seth Tobocman & Barbara Lee

"The curse of poverty has no justification in our age. It is socially as cruel and blind as the practice of cannibalism at the dawn of civilization, when men ate each other because they had not yet learned to take food from the soil or to consume the abundant animal life around them. The time has come for us to civilize ourselves by the total, direct, and immediate abolition of poverty."[9]
MARTIN LUTHER KING JR., 1967

1972: Increases in Social Security payments linked to increases in the cost of living (inflation adjustments). President Nixon proposes Family Assistance Plan to replace AFDC with a guaranteed minimum income for all families, but Congress votes it down. Supplemental Security Income (SSI) provided for low-income elders and disabled persons.

1973: The Comprehensive Employment and Training Act (CETA) promotes job training.

1975: Child support enforcement program established.

1980: President Ronald Reagan calls for sharp cuts in welfare spending.

1981: Omnibus Reconciliation Act eliminates public-service jobs and cuts benefits for the working poor, and reduces AFDC eligibility.

1987: By this date, about 40 states have some kind of workfare program.

1988: Family Support Act creates JOBS program encouraging states to enforce work requirements, but few states provide full funding.

1990: States required to cover families with 2 unemployed parents under AFDC, but tight restrictions limit eligibility. Many states begin imposing new restrictions such as "Learnfare" (sanctions against families whose children fail to attend school regularly) and family caps (no additional aid for children born to families already on assistance).

1995: Congress proposes slashing spending on public assistance programs by about 30% over the next 7 years, decentralizing AFDC through block grants, and imposing stricter time limits and work requirements on AFDC recipients.

For the past 15 years, politicians have whined that AFDC, the only cash welfare program in the U.S., discourages both work and marriage. But their real motive appears to have been cutting taxes and thereby increasing their chances of reelection. Programs suggested to improve public assistance in a positive rather than a punitive way have never received much support. In 1972, President Nixon advocated a guaranteed minimum income for all families but met substantial opposition, especially in the South (even though the minimum suggested was far below the poverty line). Instead, states chose to minimize their welfare expenditures by letting the real value of AFDC benefits decline. The federally administered Food Stamps program compensated only partly for the declining value of cash transfers. Meanwhile, expenditures on entitlement programs aimed at the nonpoor, including

Social Security and Medicare, continued to rise.

A growing emphasis on work requirements found expression in new job-training initiatives, such as the Comprehensive Employment and Training Act of 1973. Legislation passed in 1981 encouraged states to set up training and work programs; some were able to demonstrate good results for a small percentage of recipients but seldom broad-based gains. One reason: Cutbacks implemented that same year penalized the working poor, who often lost more in benefits than they could gain by earning additional wages.

Yet, conservative policy makers ignored the evidence that inadequate funding and lack of jobs imprisoned people on welfare. A much simpler—and more expedient—interpretation was that the poor lacked motivation. The 1988 Family Support Act required states to push a larger percentage of welfare recipients into training and work. When few states accomplished this task, it was decided that greater threats to recipients were needed. States began to experiment with a variety of new restrictions, requirements, and punishments.

By 1995, both Democrats and Republicans were advocating even bigger sticks to punish the poor; the only question was how hard they should be hit. The Clinton administration favored some support for poor mothers in the form of training, child care, and public employment, while Republicans and many Democrats pushed for absolute time limits and cutoffs. Both parties advocated greater autonomy for the states, which would reduce public expenditures, though the Republicans carried this further with their proposal for "no strings attached" block grants from the federal government.

Seth Tobocman & Barbara Lee

"Most women are only a husband away from welfare."[11]
VIRGINIA ANNE CARABILLO,
Vice President, National Organization of Women, 1974

"The accusation that bothers me the most is the charge that we don't care about the poor and disadvantaged."[12]
RONALD REAGAN,
President, 1980–1988

Welfare is the "umbilical cord through which the mainstream society sustains the isolated ghetto society."[13]
MICKEY KAUS, journalist, 1992

106 · WHO WAS POOR IN 1993?[14]

Poor People as a Percent of the Population

Persons	15%	People who live in central cities	22%
Children (under 18)	23%	White children	18%
Persons 65 and older	12%	Black children	46%
Married couples without children	4%	Latino children (any race)	41%
Married couples with children	9%	Highest poverty rate (Mississippi)	25%
Single mothers	46%	Lowest poverty rate (Hawaii)	8%

Poor People Compared with the Population as a Whole

27% of all people / 40% of the poor — were under age 18

12% of all people / 10% of the poor — were 65 years and older

83% of all people / 67% of the poor — were White

13% of all people / 28% of the poor — were Black

10% of all people / 21% of the poor — were Latino (any race)

25% of all people / 36% of the poor — lived in central cities

8% of all people / 28% of the poor — lived in single-mother families

81% of all families / 32% of poor families — had at least 1 member who worked at least 30 weeks during the year

64% of all families / 12% of poor families — had at least 1 year-round, full-time worker

Aid to Families with Dependent Children (AFDC)

Number of recipients	14 million
Percent of poor children not receiving AFDC	40%

Characteristics of recipients:

Children	67%
White	39%
Black	37%
Latino (any race)	18%
Mothers under 18	1%
Mothers with part-time job	4%
Mothers in school or training	17%

Average monthly benefit:

1993 ($1993)	$373
1970 ($1993)	$676
Highest monthly benefit (New York)	$703
Lowest monthly benefit (Mississippi)	$120

Food Stamps

Number of recipients	27 million
Percent of poor families who were recipients*	44%

Percent of all families receiving food stamps:

1975	8%
1993	10%
Value of maximum monthly allotment, family of 3	$295

* Data are for 1992.

Medicaid

Total persons covered	28.6 million

Percent of population covered:

Total	11%
Persons under 18	24%
Persons 65 and older	10%
Persons below poverty line	45%

Distribution of Benefits and Costs:

12% of recipients were persons 65 and older
32% of all payments were spent on

14% of recipients were disabled persons
37% of all payments were spent on

71% of all recipients were AFDC recipients
30% of all payments were spent on

HOW "WELFARE" BECAME A DIRTY WORD

Linda Gordon

In the last half-century, the American definition of "welfare" has been reversed. A term that once meant prosperity, good health, good spirits, and social respect now implies poverty, bad health, despondency, and social disrespect. A word used to describe the health of the body politic now evokes images of disease, slums, depressed single mothers, neglected children, crime, despair.

Today, welfare particularly refers to one universally maligned government program, Aid to Families with Dependent Children (AFDC), when it once referred to a vision of the good life. As we watch Congress dismantle federally-funded entitlements, it may be useful to understand how the concept of welfare became so despised.

The term welfare could logically refer to all of a government's contributions to its citizens' well-being, including provision of streets and sidewalks, schools, parks, police and fire protection, utilities, regulation of food and drugs, pollution control, building inspections, prevention of child abuse, and safe-sex education.

Even if we were to label as welfare only those programs that provide cash to citizens, we could include tax deductions for home mortgages and business expenses, farm subsidies, Medicare, and the old-age pensions provided under the Social Security Act, among many other government benefits.

The negative connotations of welfare in the United States rest on differences among the several programs originally included in the Social Security Act of 1935. The pejorative connotation attached to AFDC, a program of aid to children and single parents (almost all of whom are women), was not present when the program began. AFDC came to be viewed negatively only in the 1950s and 1960s.

The designers of the original statute did not intend to create a stratified system but rather were trying to meet different needs with different programs, all formulated under the influence of a major crisis—the Great Depression of the 1930s. The most influential drafters of the Social Security Act advocated social insurance. Seeking to prevent poverty and another depression by providing assistance to breadwinners as soon as their wages were interrupted—by unemployment, illness, or old age—they installed unemployment compensation and old-age insurance as the centerpieces of the law.

Those programs excluded the majority of Americans, although for different reasons. Blacks, who in the 1930's were still mainly agricultural and domestic workers, were effectively excluded at the insistence of Southern Democrats, who controlled crucial Congressional committees and wanted to maintain a low-wage labor force in the South. Black exclusion was the price, President Roosevelt believed, of getting the law through Congress. Most white women were excluded because the drafters assumed that the majority of them would continue to be non-employed housewives, collecting benefits as dependents on their husbands.

The program of AFDC was written by women heading the U.S. Children's Bureau, who wanted to provide for women and children who did not have a male wage earner to support them. The program was not intended to be inferior to the other Social Security programs, merely small and temporary, because its framers believed that the model of the family in which the male was the breadwinner and the female the housewife would be the standard. The framers of AFDC even believed that the causes of single motherhood—widowhood, divorce, and out-of-wedlock parenthood—would decline as economic disruption abated. Because they considered families headed by mothers to be exceptional, they designed the AFDC program very differently from the social-insurance programs:

- AFDC would be means-tested. To receive aid, an applicant would have to prove her poverty, not just initially but repeatedly, and she was required to open all her records to investigation. If she owned assets such as a house, she would be required to sell it, to impoverish herself, before she could collect a stipend, and she would lose benefits the moment she earned even a poverty wage. By contrast, a person could collect old-age or unemployment insurance (the "social insurance" programs) even if he were a millionaire.

- AFDC recipients would be morals-tested. To get assistance, an applicant would have to prove that her housekeeping, child-rearing, and sexual behavior were respectable, submitting to invasions of privacy—such as unannounced inspections of her home—that recipients of old-age and unemployment insurance escaped. The social-insurance programs were entirely automatic once you qualified; you could spend your entire pension on illegal drugs without a social worker ever inquiring about it.

- AFDC would be more a state than a federal program. With the states providing two-thirds of the money and federal matching grants providing the rest, the program was initially a federal contribution to existing state and local systems for aiding the poor. (Although the federal contribution now exceeds 50 percent in some states, the states still maintain discretion over many program rules.) The social-insurance programs, by contrast, had the cachet of newness, New Deal innovation, and exclusively federal administration, which separated them from the tradition of the dole to the poor. The current proposal, to remove the federal government entirely from setting any standards at all for aid to single parents and their children, will of course allow the states further to burden AFDC recipients with stigmatizing requirements.

- AFDC was financed by general tax revenues. Thus it appeared to be a burden on those who paid property and income taxes. By contrast, the social-insurance programs were financed by a separate payroll tax, labeled "contributions," from workers covered by them, as well as from employers. Using the term "contributions" enabled the benefits to be categorized as earned stipends or entitlements. In fact, Social Security contributions have always been mingled with general revenue, and what beneficiaries receive is not determined by what they have contributed.

- Eligibility for social-insurance benefits flowed through employment in a covered occupation. The kinds of jobs women and minority men were most likely to hold were not covered. And funding social insurance through places of employment continued a process already developing for over a century of redefining "work" to mean paid employment and to trivialize and render invisible the work that so many women did in caring for children, homes, husbands and other dependents.

This stratification created the meaning of welfare today. AFDC was stigmatized because of its differences from the other social programs, which were not usually called welfare. Originally intended to serve what in the 1930s seemed the most deserving of all needy groups—helpless mothers left alone with children by heartless men—AFDC became shameful, making its recipients undeserving by the very fact of providing for them.

The history of how these differences arose shows the deep-seated sex and race distinctions that were incorporated into the U.S. welfare state from its beginnings. Because women were considered mainly dependents, it seemed unobjectionable to design the women's welfare program to treat them as dependents of the state, while men had to be helped without eroding their dignity and head-of-household status. Because most members of minority groups were not considered full citizens, white lawmakers thought it acceptable to bar them from entitlements by excluding their jobs from coverage under the unemployment and old-age pension programs. Indeed, at first, members of minority groups were also effectively excluded from the AFDC program, because there was no federal control over racist local administrators.

Much has changed in the 60 years since the Social Security program was designed, and the changes have combined to increase the need for, and decrease the political support for, AFDC.

- As part of a groundswell of civil-rights agitation in the 1950's, black women began asserting that the right to receive welfare was one they were entitled to as citizens, just like the right to vote. The success of this claim not only increased the AFDC rolls, but also increased the proportion of blacks among AFDC recipients. Then, in the 1960s, a welfare-rights movement forced the courts to restrict the arbitrary power of states to invade recipients' privacy and cut off benefits summarily. Even more important, this activism created a more dignified image of the work of poor single mothers, reminding the public that mothering was not only work, but socially useful work. As the welfare-rights movement declined in the 1970s, however, the stigma attached to welfare intensified, strengthened now by racist animosity toward the growing number of welfare recipients from minority groups.

- The increasing number of mothers in the labor force, including middle- and upper-income women, gradually undermined the ideological basis of AFDC: the assumption that mothers should be helped to stay home with their children. This made the AFDC requirement that its beneficiaries not work for wages seem anachronistic. The recipients, not the program, were blamed.

- Increasing divorce rates left more women alone to raise their children. Despite the greater numbers who worked, many single mothers could not earn enough to support themselves and their children and pay for child care. AFDC rolls thus expanded.

- The drastic decline of industrial jobs during the last two decades not only raised unemployment rates, but also left more people chronically unemployed, underemployed, or employed only sporadically. This has meant that interruption of wages—the problem that unemployment compensation was originally designed to address—is no longer the chief cause of poverty in the United States. Many of today's unemployed are not eligible for unemployment compensation, and the parents among them turn to AFDC. The majority of AFDC recipients have been employed but are not entitled to unemployment benefits.

- Since World War II, the better jobs have carried private benefits such as health insurance, company pensions, and disability insurance—benefits that undercut support among many Americans for AFDC.

The problems of unemployment, underemployment, and employment in casual labor have helped deepen the division in our system for providing social benefits between the "middle class" (those with permanent jobs), which gets honorable, supposedly earned benefits, and the people who receive welfare. The stigma attached to welfare is self-reinforcing: The low status of its recipients stigmatizes the program, and the low status of the program stigmatizes its recipients.

The poorer and more maligned welfare recipients are, the more difficult it is for them to build political support for improving welfare. The further their benefits deteriorate, the deeper their indigence and hopelessness become. By contrast, the fact that Social Security old-age pensions were not originally classified as welfare has strengthened the lobbying power of organizations that represent older citizens, such as the American Association of Retired Persons. This has helped them maintain the level of their benefits and has reinforced their identity as citizens collecting earned entitlements.

No one likes welfare. But the idea being bandied about today that it could be abolished is misleading, a political dead end, and morally indefensible. Our goal should be to abolish poverty, not welfare. In a democracy, you can't simultaneously try to improve a public-assistance program and malign its recipients, because you have to develop popular support for trying to help them.

The Clinton administration's original welfare-reform proposal, now occluded by the even more brutal conservative proposals, started today's wave of attacks on the poor. President Clinton's rhetoric about changing welfare so as to support the values of "work and responsibility" scapegoats poor and minority mothers by implying that their problems are caused by laziness and irresponsibility, when in fact the vast majority of AFDC recipient parents are struggling valiantly to raise their children well against great obstacles.

The Clinton proposal offered nothing to alter the political, economic, and social decline of welfare recipients. It did include some changes aimed at reducing poverty, such as its call for more child-support and its proposal for subsidized and community-service jobs. But since the proposal was supposed to be "revenue-neutral," insufficient money would have been available to enable these programs to make a difference. The consistent and extreme under-funding of welfare programs since the New Deal has been a major contributor to today's politically constructed anti-welfare "public opinion."

The illusion that we have a welfare state in place then allows conservatives to blame welfare for "producing" today's escalating social problems. In fact, the federal government has never given "welfare" a serious test, all the while continuing to maintain corporate welfare—what many today call the other AFDC, Aid to Financially Dependent Corporations—funded at many tens of times what is spent on the poor.

LINDA GORDON is a historian at the University of Wisconsin–Madison. A previously published version appeared in *The Chronicle of Higher Education*, 7/20/94, pp. B1–B2.

SCAPEGOATING THE POOR

Frances Fox Piven

As the U.S. election of 1996 approaches, politicians and elected leaders of the richest country in the world are stumbling over each other in their rush to proclaim welfare America's number-one problem. Congress, the president, and the governors jostle for the initiative in promoting reforms that will eliminate federal responsibility for poor mothers and children in favor of block grants, which give the states less federal money but broader discretion to decide how that money should be spent. And should a state be inclined toward generosity, other provisions impose rigid work requirements on poor mothers and strict time limits on the receipt of aid, even while also slashing funds for child care and job training. The Medicaid program is slated for similar draconian funding cuts combined with the devolution of responsibility to the states, and so are low-income housing programs, child protection programs, nutritional programs, and so on. Meanwhile, state politicians are already proudly reporting big reductions in the welfare rolls as a result of state-level initiatives, and this at a time when child poverty is actually increasing.

What is going on? Why the uproar over these programs, which are far from being the big budget busters and which reach only a narrow stratum of the poorest Americans?

One reason is straightforward. It is greed, especially the greed of organized business and the politicians they fund. This part of the story goes back to 1981. One of President Ronald Reagan's first initiatives was a round of tax cuts skewed toward business and the affluent. The cuts were huge, reducing federal revenues by $750 billion in the first Reagan term. But the tax cuts were coupled with rapid increases in military spending. Of course, the deficit widened, which was not exactly unintentional. The hope was that the growing deficit would generate powerful pressures for reductions in spending on social programs. In the 1980s, however, Congress resisted these attempted cuts (and in 1983 went along with a Social Security tax increase that fell on working people instead).

Now, in 1996, a determined Republican leadership in Congress is proposing another round of huge tax cuts, again tilted to benefit the most affluent. This time, the plan to make up for the forfeited tax revenues with cuts in programs for the poor and the elderly is transparent.

Still, greed could not be the whole of it. After all, the politicians leading this campaign are elected. They need voter support. And the polls do show popular support, both for the attack on government in general and for the attack on programs for the poor in particular. Why are these animosities so widespread?

A thoughtful answer begins by paying attention to the discontent, anxiety, even terror generated by the enormous changes sweeping through the American economy. Wages are falling for most people despite the fact that work time is lengthening. And as the old mass-production industries contract, new and onerous forms of work are spreading. In chicken-processing or garbage-recycling plants, for example, the pace is hard and the work filthy. Sweatshops again cluster in the big older cities.

Meanwhile, inequalities are widening at a dizzying pace, as income and wealth shift away from workers to the owners and managers of capital and their corps of experts. In 1960, chief executive officers (CEOs) earned 12 times the average factory wage; by 1974, the multiplier had risen to 35; now, CEOs earn 135 times what the average factory worker earns.

Naturally, there is discontent. But why does it take such perverse form? After all, generations of pundits took for granted that voters held candidates responsible for the performance of the economy, so much so that they predicted election results from economic indicators. Why is popular ire now directed, not against poor economic performance and increased income inequality, but instead against programs that provide at least some minimum security for the most vulnerable? And why, in the 1994 election, were there such heavy Democratic losses to the Republicans who promised such program cuts, reflecting the votes of less educated whites, who are among the big losers from labor market change?

The compelling answer is the failure of political leaders, Democrats and Republicans alike, to articulate rational solutions to the economic hardships and insecurities that dominate the popular mood. The reason for this blockage in the political system is not, as is often assumed, the rise of a global economy with the threat of capital flight and low-wage competition that global markets entail. Government has not suddenly been made helpless before markets, and the American government especially is not helpless. Most other industrial nations are far more exposed to international trade and capital movements than the U.S. Yet, no other rich democratic nation has experienced the evisceration of unions, the enormous wage cuts, the slashing of the public sector, or the extremes of poverty and wealth concentration that the U.S. has experienced.

The main problem is not markets, but politics, specifically the increasing domination of money politics, reflecting the business political mobilization of the past 20 years. This domination has resulted in the revival of trade associations, the growth and proliferation of conservative think tanks, the calculated promotion of the Christian Right, the development of sophisticated propaganda and lobbying strategies, and the modernization of the Republican Party. Meanwhile, increasingly politicized business leaders also undertook a 2-decade-long assault on unions. The assault succeeded, and the resulting devastation of the unions weakened the branch of the Democratic Party that once provided something of a home for popular dissidence, leaving the political field freer for money politics.

The resulting distortions cripple Republicans and

Democrats alike. To be sure, Bill Clinton talked about economic issues in 1992; called for change, new initiatives, and so on; and went on to win the election and convene an "economic summit" at which there was a great deal of talk about reform. But then he took office, and this line of talk faded fast. Cowed by Alan Greenspan and the bond markets, President Clinton allowed his feeble economic stimulus package to fail, never pushed for a restoration of the buying power of the minimum wage, and became the champion instead of free trade and of the deregulation of international markets under the North American Free Trade Agreement (NAFTA) and the General Agreement on Tariffs and Trade (GATT). As a result, a Democratic president presided over an economic upturn in which productivity and profits moved up briskly but wages stagnated, part-time and temporary work expanded, and earnings for the less educated continued to fall.

Everywhere in the world, when people are blocked from dealing with the problems of livelihood, community, respect, and security through politics, they become more susceptible to fundamentalist appeals. When institutional reforms seem impossible, frustrated people are more likely to respond to calls for a politics of individual moral rejuvenation coupled with mobilization against vulnerable groups who are defined as the "other" and somehow to blame for the erosion of daily life.

So, too, in the U.S. popular political discourse is being led away from a preoccupation with wages and jobs, which had been taken for granted as the dominant issues of electoral politics since the New Deal, to a politics of individual responsibility and "values." At the same time, popular anger is increasingly directed against minorities and the poor, especially poor women, whose transgressions of core values are said to be somehow responsible for contemporary troubles. That is why welfare and the out-of-wedlock mothers presumably encouraged by welfare to have babies, have come to figure so largely in public discourse.

Of course, politicians also make more reasoned arguments to smooth the way for this sort of scapegoat politics. It will actually be good for the poor, the argument goes, to slash the programs that give them aid because these programs generate perverse incentives. With a welfare check in sight, we are told, people give up the effort to be self-reliant and fall into a torpor called dependency. Or, even worse, they have babies to make certain the checks come and keep coming. These arguments are powerful because they evoke prejudices embedded in American culture—against the poor, against sexualized women, against minorities. But they are also based on a campaign of misinformation that has shaped popular understandings and fueled ancient prejudices.

FRANCES FOX PIVEN is a political scientist at the City University of New York.

FEDERAL IRRESPONSIBILITY, DISUNITED STATES

The deficit is to be eliminated by the year 2002—but not by any shared sacrifice. Even as the poor, elderly and students must prepare to give up hundreds of billions of dollars in federal-program support from now until 2002, tax prefer-

ences—mostly for corporations and the richest 25% of American families—are scheduled to grow by about a third and to total about $3.5 trillion over the next seven years. Packaged as "deficit reduction," this has become one of the decades biggest rip-offs.[16]

KEVIN PHILLIPS, author and former
Republican political consultant

The rip-off designed by Congress in 1995 includes reductions of funding and the restructuring of programs that could affect over 25 million low-income Americans. Sweeping proposed changes include cuts in student loans and grants; slashes in programs that provide housing, food, and heat to low-income families; and reductions in the Earned Income Tax Credit that will increase the taxes of 17 million low-income workers. Federal changes to Aid to Families with Dependent Children (AFDC) would eliminate virtually all assurances and safeguards for poor mothers and their children, while cuts in Medicaid spending reduce health care spending and coverage for low-income families.

The spending reductions would begin gradually and increase over the next 5 to 7 years. Cuts to AFDC and Medicaid, the two largest programs that assist the poor, account for 25% of the proposed 7-year, $1 trillion deficit-reduction plan. The Clinton administration calculates that the changes in AFDC will push over 1.1 million more children into poverty.[17]

Block Grants: Passing the Buck
If Congress succeeds, AFDC and Medicaid will no longer be administered by the federal government. Instead, funds will be transferred to the states in the form of block grants. This means that states will have a fixed amount of money to spend on public assistance. If they run out, poor families will be left to fend for themselves. States will be able to deny federal cash benefits to parents not participating in work or training programs after 2 years of receiving welfare. They will also be able to end cash assistance altogether and/or turn the administration of block grants over to private agencies. There are no assurances that poor parents will receive the childcare assistance they need in order to work outside the home or attend school. Families that have received welfare for more than five years will no longer be eligible for AFDC.

Supporters of the block grant approach argue that it gives states more flexibility and decision-making power. But it typically results in spending cuts: Of the 9 programs President Ronald Reagan turned into block grants in the early 1980s, 7 received less funding in 1993 than they did in 1983 (when adjusted for inflation).[18] The new federal block grant plan freezes AFDC funding at 1994 levels through the year 2000, with only small adjustments for population growth. It also limits growth in Medicaid spending to 4% a year after 1998, which is less than the expected rate of increase in health-care costs.

States do not need block grants in order to gain more flexibility. They already have enormous leeway in implementing AFDC and Medicaid. The Social Security Act of 1935 gave states the option of requesting waivers that would allow them to experiment with departures from federal provisions. Few states requested AFDC waivers until the 1980s, when some began implementing provisions emphasizing paid work for single mothers. In the early 1990s, as the political battles over welfare heated up, more state legislatures and governors began promoting welfare reform, and the Clinton administration actively encouraged them to experiment. Between 1992 and 1995, 42 states were granted permission to experiment with one or more policy alternatives aimed at promoting work, schooling, marriage, and child immunization and at deterring child-bearing, teenage school truancy, and immigration.

The new block grant system will actually reduce flex-ibility by imposing new rules. States will be required to reduce family assistance when paternity has not been established and to deny family assistance when a parent has not cooperated in establishing paternity (in the past, only five states ever requested waivers for such provi-sions). States will be compelled to impose time limits (only 11 states ever requested that provision).[19]

Will States Do a Better Job Helping the Poor?

The answer to this question depends on which state and under what political conditions. States have the latitude to make drastic cuts. They have never been—and are still not—required by law to raise poor families' standard of living. Nor are they required to consult with poor people or their advocates regarding the effects of program changes. Most state policy initiatives have been designed to kick poor people off the rolls and reduce social spending.

Many states have also tried using carrots rather than sticks, increasing the positive incentives for poor people to find paid employment and increase their savings. Between 1992 and 1995, 34 states changed their welfare laws to allow recipients to keep more of their benefits when they earn income and to increase the limit of cash assets (the standard is $1,000) they are allowed to have without losing eligibility. In addition, 32 states chose to provide greater benefits to 2-parent families, and 21 states extended the length of time recipients could remain eligible for Medicaid after entering paid employment.

At the same time, many states also applied for waivers to implement provisions designed to curtail recipients' benefits and rights. Work requirements and time limits were imposed in 28 states. Plans to deny aid to AFDC families if children fail to attend school were approved in 25 states, and family caps that deny benefits for any child born to an AFDC recipient were imposed by 18 states.[20]

State policies are likely to become more restrictive under a block grant system for several reasons. Matching money for state funding for job training and childcare programs that allow mothers to enter paid employment will no longer be provided. Even when matching funds were available, states failed to utilize them fully. As feder-al funds slated for such programs are reduced, states will be even more reluctant to fork over their own revenues.

Recessions or even small economic downturns send state fiscal ledgers into a tizzy. If business profits fall, firms begin to lay off workers. As unemployment increases, so does poverty. People consume less because they are earn-ing less or are more fearful of losing their jobs. Sales tax receipts drop as people buy fewer things, especially big-ticket items such as cars and appliances. Just as the pover-ty caseload rises, state tax revenues fall. Because states are legally required to balance their budgets, declining tax revenues force them to cut spending even though more people need assistance.

The way states handled public assistance during the recession of 1991–1992 does not augur well for the future. They slashed their entirely state-funded General Assistance (GA) programs, the last resort for poor people ineligible for AFDC or Supplemental Security Income. Of the 28 states with statewide programs, 22 reduced benefits, restricted eligibility, or eliminated their programs altogether.[21] In addition, 9 states cut basic AFDC benefits.[22]

Problems with the existing waiver system are likely to worsen under the block grant structure. Unrestricted state authority to limit assistance could provoke a competitive "race to the bottom." If one state imposes particularly strict time limits, policy makers in neighboring states will feel pressure to follow suit to minimize the possibility of attracting poor migrants. In the absence of federal oversight, extreme welfare cuts in one state could spread throughout the country.[23]

Back to the Future

New legislation would almost certainly increase the number of people, especially children, living in poverty. Cuts in nutrition and housing programs will increase hunger and homelessness. AFDC time limits will result in complete elimination of aid for many needy families. Reductions in Medicaid will make it harder for the poor to get adequate health care. More restricted access to student grants and loans will deny low-income students the opportunity to go to college thus reducing the productivity of an entire generation.

Paid employment will do little to help those shoved off the welfare rolls. Low-wage jobs, the only ones AFDC recipients and other poor adults are likely to find, will do little to alleviate poverty, especially with cuts in the Earned Income Tax Credit. Forcing an estimated 1 million additional adults into the labor market will either increase unemployment or depress the earnings of all low-wage workers.

The New Deal programs of the 1930s successfully lifted millions out of economic despair. The War on Poverty declared in the 1960s decreased poverty and infant mortality. Legislation designed in 1995 promises to undo virtually all these gains in a very short period of time.

The poor and their advocates must now take the fight for better public assistance to every state legislature as well as to the nation's capitol. The sheer complexity of this task will make it difficult. Still, decentralization may open up new opportunities. State electoral campaigns are less costly than congressional ones. Grassroots organizations can combat affluent lobbyists more effectively at the local than at the national level. Conservatives may come to regret the new federalism.

The job will not be easy, but there are historical precedents. Both old-age assistance and aid to single-parent families with dependent children emerged on the state level between 1900 and 1920, providing an important model for New Deal legislation in the 1930s. Another long fight will be necessary to achieve progressive state policies designed to help rather than punish the poor.

See p. 142 for abbreviations used in notes.

1. For overviews of legislation during these years, see Theda Skocpol, *Protecting Soldiers and Mothers: The Political Origins of Social Policy in the United States* (Cambridge: Harvard University Press, 1992); and Linda Gordon, *Pitied but Not Entitled: Single Mothers and the History of Welfare* (New York: The Free Press, 1994).

2. Lewis D. Eigen and Jonathan P. Siegel, *The Macmillan Dictionary of Political Quotations* (New York: Macmillan, 1993), p. 704.

3. Josephine Shaw Lowell, *Public Relief and Private Charity* (New York: G.P. Putnam's Sons, 1884), p. 58.

4. Eigen and Siegel, p. 530.

5. For overviews of legislation during these years, see Mimi Abramowitz, *Regulating the Lives of Women. Social Welfare Policy from Colonial Times to the Present* (Boston: South End Press, 1988); and Jill Quadagno, *The Color of Welfare. How Racism Undermined the War on Poverty* (New York: Oxford University Press, 1994).

6. Eigen and Siegel, p. 532.

7. Eigen and Siegel, p. 534.

8. Eigen and Siegel, p. 532.

9. Eigen and Siegel, p. 533.

10. For overviews of legislation during these years see *Congressional Digest* (June–July 1995); and Kenneth Jost, "Welfare Reform: Should Welfare Benefits Be Used to Change Recipients' Behavior?" *Congressional Quarterly Research* 2, no. 44 (April 10, 1992), 313–36.

11. Eigen and Siegel, p. 704.

12. Ronald Reagan, "Remarks at a White House Luncheon for Black Clergymen," March 26, 1982, *The Public Papers of the Presidents of the United States: Ronald Reagan* (Washington, DC: GPO, 1989), p. 383.

13. Mickey Kaus, *The End of Equality* (New York: Basic Books, 1992), p.117.

14. *Current Population Survey,* March 1994.

15. This table covers the three major federal welfare programs in effect in 1995. Source: *Current Population Survey*; March 1994; *SA 1994*; David E. Rosenbaum, "Welfare: Who Gets It? How Much Does It Cost?" *NYT*, 3/23/95, p. A23. Highest and lowest AFDC benefits based on data from the 48 contiguous states.

16. Kevin Phillips, "On a Collision Course" *LAT*, 10/29/95, p. M6.

17. Elizabeth Shogren, "Welfare Report Clashes with Clinton, Senate" *LAT*, 10/27/95 pp. A1, A14.

18. Steven Gold, "The ABCs of Block Grants," *State Fiscal Brief,* no. 28, (Albany, N.Y.: Center for Study of the States, Nelson A. Rockefeller Institute of Government, March 1995), p. 2.

19. This includes waivers from January 1992 through October 1995. Center for Law and Social Policy, *Updated Waiver Information* (Washington, DC, October 1995).

20. Center for Law and Social Policy, *Updated Waiver Information.*

21. Center on Budget and Policy Priorities, *States and the Poor: How Budget Decisions Affect Low-Income Families* (Washington, DC, February 1993), pp. 35–36.

22. Center on Budget and Policy Priorities and Center for the Study of the States, *The States and the Poor: How Budget Decisions in 1991 Affected Low–Income People* (Washington DC and Albany, N.Y., December 1991), pp. viii–ix.

23. Steve Savner and Mark Greenberg, *The CLASP Guide to Welfare Waivers: 1992–1995* (Washington DC, Center for Law and Social Policy, May 23, 1995), p. 6.

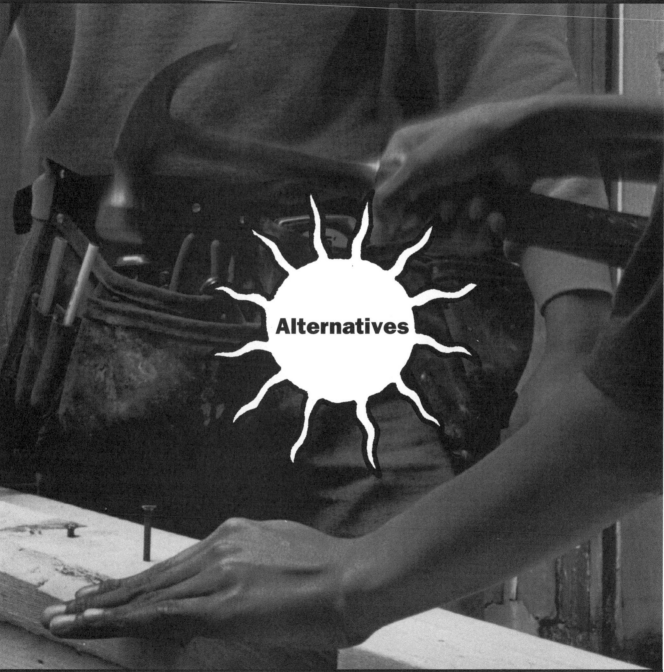

Alternatives

Mark Pokempner / Impact Visuals

The conservative attack on public assistance has largely silenced discussion of progressive alternatives to the current welfare system. We believe that it is important to listen to the voices of local welfare rights organizations, which include many low-income citizens with firsthand knowledge of life under the poverty line. In spite of enormous opposition, these organizations continue to articulate a radical vision of an economy that would provide a safe and secure livelihood for everyone. In Massachusetts, the Coalition for Basic Human Needs (CBHN) has lobbied for a simple program that includes (1) guaranteed income for all families, (2) guaranteed child care for all income-eligible families, (3) guaranteed health care for all families, (4) a living wage, (5) increased education and training opportunities, and (6) increased efficiency of child support enforcement services. Taken as a whole, this package may seem like wishful thinking. But many social scientists make a persuasive case for more serious attention to some or all of these measures. We have selected four short articles, spanning the progressive political spectrum, that outline alternative visions of welfare reform.

A copy of CBHN's legislative program can be obtained from them at 54 Essex Street, Cambridge, MA 02139, 617-497-0126. For a listing of other welfare rights organizations, see Chapter 9.

Mark Pokempner / Impact Visuals

WELFARE AS WE NEED IT

Theda Skocpol and William Julius Wilson

President Clinton has eloquently renewed his promise to "end welfare as we know it." Now, as his aides hammer out legislation to keep that promise, he needs to insist on policies that truly further the widely shared values he laid out in his State of the Union Message: work and parental responsibility.

What it will take is clear. Jobs must be available to all adults who can work, and they must have wages, benefits and protections that are suitable for families. Policies must require and enable parents to devote time and money to the care of children. These things can be done without huge amounts of new public resources.

The Administration wants states to turn welfare offices into "transitional" centers for training and job placement. Since most poor men and women want to work, they will welcome this change. We urge the President to make the commitment to work iron-clad by helping local governments create public jobs when private-sector jobs are lacking. But in making the shift toward work rather than welfare, the Administration needs to make two fundamental breaks with past policies.

First, work should be defined to include parental time spent with children. The President's call for responsible parenthood cannot be realized with the policies his planners are contemplating, because they are based on an unrealistic and unfair premise—that impoverished single mothers should be required to do full-time wage work rather than to combine part-time employment with care for children, as many more privileged American mothers still do.

Second, it would be a mistake to leave in place the unwieldy and inefficient state-by-state system of collecting child support from absent parents (mostly divorced or unwed fathers). "Deadbeat dads" owe $34 billion a year in uncollected child support. If this money were efficiently collected and delivered to custodial parents, the economic security of America's children would be vastly improved.

This is not a welfare issue so much as a matter of preventing poverty in the first place. One in two children will grow up at least part of the time in a single-parent family, and such families are likely to fall into poverty.

What we need is a national system of child support that works automatically, and without the stigma attached to the current system. Both parents must be identified by their Social Security numbers at the birth of each child. Later, if a divorce occurs or if a parent is otherwise absent, then he (or more rarely, she) would be liable for a tax, depending on the number of children involved.

Child support would be collected like Social Security and other payroll taxes. If the noncustodial parent's income goes up, he automatically pays more; if it goes down, he pays less. No parent could move out of state to avoid such a national tax. Efficient child support enforcement would make it unattractive for men to father and abandon multiple families, so this system might well encourage stable marriages.

As with Social Security, there would be a minimum child support benefit if the absent parent's tax payment went down too far. It could be set at about the level of a half-time minimum-wage job.

This would be very different from welfare. A divorced or unwed mother could not live on a minimum benefit; she would have to work at least half time. If she chose to work more, she and her child would get ahead, because the minimum benefit would not be taken away.

But suppose the mother decided to spend part of each day with her children. This could be vital for a poor family in a tough neighborhood. After all, it is exactly such single mothers who most need time to visit school, meet with other parents in voluntary organizations or be at home when the child returns from school. Poor families and neighborhoods need both the discipline of work and the time to build social networks and cohesion.

Since its inception, the terrible flaw in the U.S. welfare system has been its failure to support efforts to combine employment and child-rearing. Back in the 1910's, "mothers' pensions" sought to keep impoverished mothers out of the wage labor force and entirely at home with their children (although they were never given enough money actually to live that way). It would be a shame, in the 1990's, to go in an equally unrealistic way to the opposite extreme, forcing poor mothers into full-time low-wage jobs. This is not the right ideal for public policy to uphold.

Part-time jobs combined with child support would also be less costly than finding full-time jobs for millions of current welfare recipients.

To be sure, the Administration is promoting measures to help poor families. A big step was taken last summer with the expansion of the earned-income tax credit.

Wisely, the Administration now wants to pay this wage supplement throughout the year, so families can count on it as regular income. It also wants to expand child-care subsidies for working parents.

Health insurance is equally crucial. As a Chicago welfare mother who wants to "go out there and get a job" put it: "I don't like being on public aid right now. But without a medical card, what do I do when my kids get sick?" If the Clinton forces lose in Congress to proponents of the upper-middle-class-oriented Cooper plan,* then many low-wage workers will be left uninsured and it will be hard for parents to move off welfare. For the sake of welfare reform as well as economic efficiency, the President's promise to veto any bill that falls short of universal coverage is wise.

Let's use this round of policy changes to say to all American fathers and mothers: "You must support your children through a combination of work and time spent with them." Government will help working families. If marriages fail, public policies will enforce and sustain responsibility for both parents—without pretending that single mothers can be expected to carry the burdens of two parents at once.

*A health care bill proposed by Rep. Jim Cooper (D–Tennessee) in 1993 and 1994 that emphasized competition and did require employers to pay for health insurance.

THEDA SKOCPOL is a sociologist at Harvard University, and WILLIAM JULIUS WILSON is a sociologist at University of Chicago. Previously published in *New York Times*, 2/9/94, p. A20.

A WELFARE REFORM PROGRAM BASED ON HELP FOR WORKING PARENTS

Barbara Bergmann and Heidi Hartmann

We do need welfare reform, but the kind advocated in the Republican Contract with America will push American children deeper into poverty. It would be immoral to reduce the standard of living of already-poor children or tear them away from their mothers, as the Republicans propose, with the purpose of deterring other women from new pregnancies.

We should enact a welfare reform that encourages job-holding and sustains working parents and their children in decency; it would be based on the concept of Help for Working Parents (HWP). The 2 keys to such a reform are help with health insurance and child care. Those now on AFDC get their health insurance and child care needs provided for. It is brutally difficult for families with access only to low-wage jobs to survive on welfare unless these two are provided. If they are provided, then a year-round, full-time job at the minimum wage would keep a mother and 2 children in decency, if supplemented by the Earned Income Tax Credit and Food Stamp programs we already have, as well as an expanded housing assistance program, especially for families in high-rent areas.

Data suggest that many women currently receiving welfare want to work. With the assistance proposed here, they would be able to get a fair share of the jobs that do exist (even if the unemployment rate increases as more women enter the labor market). Most already have a high-school diploma and several years of work experience; but inadequate child care and inadequate health care benefits on the jobs they can get have slowed their progress. Data also show that women who have jobs want fewer births than women who stay home. Through working, these mothers can provide a higher standard of living for the children they already have.

Under the HWP program, low-income 2-parent families would get the same help as single-parent families, and families would not have to go on welfare to qualify. There would be a fallback package of benefits and cash assistance for parents out of jobs. Research suggests that a considerable proportion of single parents would leave AFDC in response to the new possibility of living decently without welfare, but those whose employability problems are too severe would continue to need long-term income support.

The cost of this program would depend on how many welfare clients became employed. If 60% of them did, the program would cost $86 billion a year in new spending, which could be financed by shifting funds from now-superfluous defense activities, the CIA, and agricultural subsidies to wealthy farmers. Alternatively, taxes on the better-off could be raised to provide the needed revenue.

We advocate a Help for Working Parents (HWP) Welfare reform package that would:

1. Guarantee health insurance to all families with children. (Additional cost: $29 billion; would cover all currently uninsured families with children.)

2. Provide child care for preschool children and after-

school care for older children at no cost to families in the bottom 20% and at sliding scale fees to middle-class families. These facilities should get children ready for school, and should teach non-violence, tolerance, honesty, and self-reliance. (Additional cost: $54 billion; assumes money currently spent on half-day programs would be used to fund some of the full-day costs.)

3. Provide more housing assistance to families with children, especially in high-rent areas. (Additional cost: $8.2 billion.)

4. Maintain current cash assistance (equivalent to AFDC) for single parents who do not work and extend and expand it to all low-income parents who are out of the labor force or unemployed as a cash fallback. (Saving over current AFDC and food stamp costs, based on 60% shift to the labor market: $19.6 billion.)

Other costs of the program would result from increases in the cost of the Earned Income Tax Credit and Unemployment Insurance, as the number of working families receiving help grows.

Additional revenue both to the government and to families could come from more rigorous enforcement of child support obligations, under a Child Support Assurance program for mothers willing to establish paternity. We have not, however, calculated the costs of generating this revenue; we believe the increased collection effort would more than pay for itself through increased revenues.

HEIDI HARTMANN is an economist and President of the Institute for Women's Policy Research. **BARBARA BERGMANN** is an economist at American University. A previously published, but revised, version appeared in *Feminist Economics* 1, no. 2 (Summer 1995): 85–89.

ESTIMATION OF COST FOR CURRENT PROGRAMS HELPING LOW-INCOME FAMILIES WITH CHILDREN, AND PROPOSED
HELP-FOR-WORKING-PARENTS (HWP) WELFARE REFORM PROGRAM

	1994 PROGRAM	HWP PROGRAM	DIFFERENCE
COSTS FOR FAMILIES WITHOUT A PARENT IN LABOR FORCE			
Number of Families (millions)	4.7	2.0	-2.7
AFDC	$25.3	-	-$25.3
Food Stamps	11.5	4.9	-6.6
Job Training for AFDC clients	1.0	-	-1.0
Housing Assistance	6.0	6.9	+0.9
Medical Care	24.3	10.3	-14.0
Child Care	13.6	19.0	+5.4
Cash Fallback	-	10.8	+10.8
Total, families without a parent in labor force	$81.7	$51.9	-$29.8
COSTS FOR FAMILIES WITH PARENT(S) IN LABOR FORCE*			
Number of Families (millions)	2.3	5.0	2.7
Cost of Programs (billions of $):			
EITC	10.3	22.5	+12.2
Food Stamps	2.2	4.7	+2.5
Housing Assistance	3.4	7.3	+3.9
Medical Care	10.3	53.6	+43.3
Child Care	12.6	61.3	+48.7
Unemployment Insurance	.5	1.5	+1.0
Cash Fallback	-	4.5	+4.5
Total, families with parent(s) in labor force	39.3	155.4	+116.1
GRAND TOTAL	$121	$207.3	$+86.3

*Includes families with children from the 20% of lowest-income families in the United States and 60% of former AFDC families projected to be in the labor force.

NOTE: Estimates are based on 1991 magnitudes, escalated by 10% to approximate 1994 levels.

EITC cost is from U.S. Department of the Treasury, *Statistics of Income Bulletin* 12, no. 4 (Spring 1993): 12. Kindergarten spending data were derived from material in National Center for Education Statistics, *Digest of Education Statistics*, 1993 (Lanham, MD, 1993). The remainder were derived from U.S. Bureau of the Census, *Statistical Abstract of the United States*, 1993 (Washington, DC, 1993) and Congressional Research Service, "Cash and Noncash Benefits for Persons with Limited Income: Eligibility Rules, Recipient and Expenditure Data, FY 1990–92, " no. 93-382, (Washington, DC: Congressional Research Service, 1993). An explanation of the estimates for the HWP program may be obtained by writing to: CPE, Box 785, Amherst, MA 01004. The original version of this proposal suggested that a fallback package for those not in jobs might consist mostly of vouchers. Bergmann and Hartmann were subsequently convinced by those commenting on the proposal that the gain in political acceptability from vouchering did not outweigh the disadvantages in terms of status loss to clients of the program and administrative hassle of the vouchering approach.

CUT WELFARE BY PAY-EQUITY REFORM

June Lapidus and Deborah M. Figart

The so-called "two years and out" facet of the Clinton administration's welfare reform plan requiring welfare recipients to obtain paid employment or perform community service after a period of two years, may be an admirable goal—but it will not improve economic conditions for women and children until all women are paid wages that are sufficient to support a family.

Just because a woman obtains a job does not mean she is exiting poverty. Jobs with high concentrations of women pay less than jobs that are predominant male. Fifty-five percent of all women and 62% of working poor women are in jobs that are at least 70% female. It is reasonable to assume, therefore, that women who enter the labor market as a result of any welfare reform plan are also likely to be employed in low-paying, predominantly female jobs.

Our research, and that of other labor economists, demonstrates that for each 1% increase in the number of women in an occupation, wages decrease by at least .11%. This wage penalty for working in a female-dominated occupation has serious effects for women and their families. Over one-fourth of women in female-dominated occupations earn less than the hourly wage necessary to bring a family of three above the federal poverty threshold—$5.65 an hour or $11,000 a year.

The penalty for working in female-dominated jobs could be eliminated if the nation adopted a policy called comparable worth. Our research indicates that comparable worth would reduce the percent of working women earning below poverty level wages by approximately 40%. For female-dominated occupations such as clerical work, the results would be even more dramatic. Poverty among clerical workers would decrease by over 74%.

Comparable worth is a specific pay equity strategy predicated on the assertion that occupational segregation has led to the systematic undervaluation of work done by women, and that this undervaluation is reflected in lower market wages. Since men and women often do not perform substantially "equal work" according to the Equal Pay Act of 1963, comparable worth is considered "equal pay for work of equal value" to an employer.

Comparable worth attempts to correct the undervaluation of female-dominated occupations by eliminating bias within an individual employer's compensation plan. By using techniques such as evaluating jobs by standardized criteria, assigning points for compensable job characteristics and translating job evaluation point scores into new, unbiased salary ranges, the systematic undervaluation of women's work can be reversed.

For example, the predominantly female occupation of maid has a median weekly wage of $245 while the predominantly male occupation of janitor has a median weekly wage of $303. A comparable worth study would measure the skills, training demands, working conditions, degree of responsibility and effort in the two occupations to determine whether the difference is due to job characteristics or is partly a result of the occupations being sex segregated. If the wage differences were found not to result from actual job characteristics, the wages of the maids would be adjusted upward. (The Equal Pay Act states that no one's wages can be lowered as a result of remedies for prior discrimination.)

Pay equity is typically achieved through legislation, collective bargaining or litigation. It was implemented first in Australia in 1975. Five Canadian provinces have passed pay equity legislation. Minnesota, Iowa, Washington, New York, Oregon and Wisconsin already have implemented pay equity. Dozens of municipalities, counties and school districts have also eliminated sex bias from their pay systems, leading directly to new salary ranges as well as wage increases for female-dominated job classes. Cities such as Philadelphia and Washington have investigated how people of color, in addition to women, are paid.

Pay equity has progressed in the private sector, mainly through voluntary efforts by management, labor-management cooperation at the bargaining table, or as a last resort, litigation. Private sector efforts include those at newspapers, colleges and universities, and at large employers such as General Electric, some hospitals managed by Kaiser and AT&T as well as several of the "Baby Bells."

The cost of comparable-worth implementation has varied from employer to employer, but generally public employers have spent an average of 1% of payroll to eliminate gender bias from their evaluation and compensation systems.

In a survey of employers by the National Committee on Pay Equity, one surprising result was the lack of concern about cost. Few private employers were distressed about a negative impact on profitability. This may well be because pay equity boosts the morale of those who feel they have been undervalued and underpaid. Many labor economists and personnel directors understand that an increase in employee morale can boost productivity. As a result, a pay-equity wage increase might pay for itself.

It is also important to note that taxpayers are already paying significant costs for not implementing comparable worth. Wages in female-dominated occupations are so low that some workers are eligible for Food Stamps, housing subsidies and Earned Income tax credits. Those costs represent nothing less than government subsidies to low-wage employers.

Some object to the implementation of comparable worth because they believe it interferes with the free market system. Yet it is an already established legal and political principle that employers do not have the right to discriminate based on sex. Depressed wages for those engaged in primarily female occupations is clearly a form of sex discrimination.

In order for a move off welfare to also mean a move out of poverty, labor market reform must accompany welfare reform. Until then, calls for time limits on welfare may succeed in reducing welfare rolls, but we should not fool ourselves into thinking we are improving the lives of women and children.

JUNE LAPIDUS is an economist at Roosevelt University, and DEBORAH M. FIGART is an economist at Eastern Michigan University. Previously published in *Chicago Tribune*, 7/26/94, p. 13.

WHY WE NEED A GUARANTEED MINIMUM INCOME

Cyann Brolfe

So-called social programs in this country do not work. They do not lift people out of poverty, they do not treat people with respect, and they do not make good use of taxpayers' money. We should stop trying to defend them from conservative attacks and push instead for a program we can believe in. We need to fight for a guaranteed minimum income for everyone.

No more Aid to Families with Dependent Children, no more Food Stamps, no more Social Security, no more veterans' benefits, no more Earned Income Tax Credit, no more red tape, no more long lines, no more small print. We should just grant every person who is a citizen of our country a minimum income of $8,000 a year. Children could be guaranteed a minimum of $4,000 a year, payable to parents or caregivers, until they reach age 18. All grants should be indexed to the rate of inflation so that their real value remains the same.

Think of it as a kind of inheritance, a share of the family business, a citizenship dividend. The basic idea was proposed over 200 years ago by Thomas Paine, one of the strongest advocates of our first War of Independence. The concept has popped up several times since then, in many European countries and in legislation proposed by President Richard Nixon in the 1960s.

A guaranteed minimum income, combined with nationally funded health care, would provide a simple, sturdy safety net for everyone. It would give people a choice between not working for pay and living very simply or working for pay and enjoying a much higher level of consumption. Also, it would enable adults to go back to school and acquire new skills that can increase their access to more interesting or lucrative work. Some people might choose to reduce their hours of paid work or to work for several years in a highly paid job and then take an education break.

We could combine the minimum guaranteed income with changes in the tax system designed to finance it. All existing income and payroll taxes (including Social Security) could be replaced by a flat tax of 30% on all income earned (wages, interest, profits, and capital gains). For example, individuals who worked full-time, year-round at the minimum wage would each get their minimum income ($8,000) plus earnings of $8,840 minus 30% of those earnings (they would pay $2,652 in taxes) for a total of $14,188 a year.

Single parents raising a child under age 6 without working for pay would receive $8,000 a year for themselves, and $4,000 a year for each child for a minimum of $12,000 per year. Individuals with no children earning $26,667 a year would get the basic income of $8,000 and would pay about the same amount in taxes on their earned income (30% of $26,667 is about $8,000). Beyond this income level, they would pay more in taxes than they received in benefits.

A married couple with 1 child would receive a guaranteed income of $20,000 ($8,000 plus $8,000 plus $4,000). The income level at which such a family would pay more in taxes than it received in benefits would be

$66,666. This tax and benefit structure would redistribute income from rich to poor and from nonparents to parents. It would reward both parental labor and market labor. It would also be much easier to administer than the current system.

What if everyone decides just to goof off? Not likely. Studies show that people who work outside the market economy (primarily women) work just as many hours, if not more, than those who work primarily for pay. Most people will probably want to work not just in order to earn more but also because the kinds of jobs they will be able to choose from will be more rewarding.

The guaranteed minimum income will make it difficult for employers to find people willing to do unpleasant, unskilled, low-paid work. But in our economy, there are not enough jobs to go around anyway. A labor shortage would increase employers' incentives to develop new productive technologies to benefit consumers without creating new insecurities for workers.

How much would this program cost? It is hard to say. More money would go to the poor, but less would go to the rich. More money would go to parents and children; about the same amount would go to the elderly. We might see a reduction in time devoted to market work but a big improvement in both educational levels and overall standard of living. If there were a shortfall of government revenues that could not be met by cuts in other parts of the budget, such as military spending and corporate subsidies, we could consider two supplementary ways of reducing costs and raising money: (1) a basic community–service requirement of as much as 20 hours a week for those receiving a basic income but not working for pay, raising children, or caring for other dependents, and (2) a wealth tax (with no loopholes) that would limit to $200,000 the values of money or assets an individual could bequeath to any one individual.

No matter how it is financed, many people will object to the idea of a guaranteed basic income. Those who earn high salaries or expect to inherit large amounts of money will complain that they do not want to support any dependents except their own children. But a nation is like a family: It cannot survive in a world based purely on market competition and individual choice. We should enforce collective responsibilities and obligations to care for one another. We should reward nonmarket work and encourage people to invest in their own skills. We should make the health and welfare of our fellow citizens our first priority.

Conservative welfare reform is a systematic form of domestic violence that threatens to throw many of us into the streets. The only way to fight back is to create a new kind of shelter in which we can all feel safe. We cannot do that without a guaranteed minimum income for all.

CYANN BROLFE is the pen name of an economist and journalist committed to the welfare rights movement.

Resources

Alain McLaughlin / Impact Visuals

A GUIDE TO MAJOR PUBLIC SUPPORT PROGRAMS FOR LOW–INCOME HOUSEHOLDS

All the programs listed in this section were established over the past 60 years to assist low-income households. Each one, except the Women, Infants, and Children's program, was profoundly threatened by the Republican-led Congress in 1995. Major funding cuts were proposed for some, such as low-income energy assistance, Pell grants, and housing programs. Others, such as the Legal Services Corporation and summer youth employment, were slated for complete elimination. Still other programs were restructured to revoke previous funding promises and severely reduce eligibility; these include Aid to Families with Dependent Children (AFDC), Medicaid, and the Earned Income Tax Credit.

As this book went to press, the official 1996 budget had not been signed. However, the writing was on the wall, both houses of Congress had agreed on the major parameters of cuts and restructuring. Here is a summary of programs as they existed in the fall of 1995.

CASH INCOME PROGRAMS

Aid to Families with Dependent Children (AFDC). The AFDC program offers cash assistance to poor families with children. Eligibility standards are stipulated by each state, with the federal government setting broad rules. The program has always been directed primarily toward women raising children without male support. The federal government paid 55% of those benefits; the states paid the rest.

Supplemental Security Income (SSI). In 1972, Congress replaced the various federal and state programs that served low-income elders and disabled persons with SSI. This federally funded program guarantees income to people who are blind, disabled, or at least 65 years old who have limited assets (no more than $2,000 for individuals and $3,000 for couples) and who have incomes below certain levels. The federal government pays the full cost of the guarantees, which are adjusted annually for inflation, based on changes in the Consumer Price Index. States may supplement the federal guarantee at their own expense; about half did so in 1995.

General Assistance (GA). These programs are funded entirely by states to provide cash assistance to low-income persons and families. Funds from GA may serve those who do not qualify for federal support but who still need help. Payment levels and eligibility criteria are established by states. Typically, GA programs are smaller and shorter in duration than the federal programs.

Earned Income Tax Credit (EITC). The federal EITC, established in 1975, is a refundable tax credit to low-income families. The credit depends on the number of children in the family and on the family's total income. The EITC is intended to help poor and low-income working families avoid poverty or limit the extent of their poverty when they work in very low-wage jobs.

FOOD BENEFITS

Food Stamps. In 1964, Congress passed the Food Stamp Act, which provides low-income households with coupons (worth up to $0.78 per person per meal) that they can use like cash to purchase food products. Participating households are expected to use 30% of their monthly cash income for food purchases, and monthly Food Stamp allotments make up the difference between a recipient's expected contribution to food costs and an amount judged to be sufficient to buy a minimally adequate low-cost diet. The federal government pays the full cost of Food Stamps.

Women, Infants, and Children Food and Nutrition Information Program (WIC). Established in 1974, WIC is funded primarily by the federal government, though a few states also contribute revenue. It provides poor women and children with vouchers for certain food items, nutrition counseling, and referrals to other programs. Eligibility is set by the federal government. WIC is not an entitlement and is provided only if and when funds are available. Many states have waiting lists for potential recipients.

School Lunch and Breakfast Programs. These nutrition programs were established in 1946. Poor school-age children in public or private nonprofit schools are eligible for free or reduced-priced breakfast, lunch, or milk. The program also provides meals for poor adults and children in day-care programs. The federal government provides most of the funding. States pay $0.07 per meal served. Approximately 50% of all school-age youths participate.

MEDICAL CARE

Medicaid. Medicaid was established in 1965 as Title XIX of the Social Security Act to provide health care to extremely poor families that meet eligibility requirements. Each state develops and administers its own Medicaid program and provides health care to low-income families with children as well as to elderly and disabled people whose high medical costs exceed their income. The federal and state governments share the costs of the program.

Maternal and Child Health Services. The Maternal and Child Health block grant covers over 30 programs that promote care for women and children. Services include care for children with special needs, prenatal care, pregnancy and birth care, home visits, primary physical care, and school-based services. Clients are charged a fee based on their ability to pay.

EDUCATIONAL AID

Head Start. Launched in 1965 as a comprehensive child-development program for low-income children and families, Head Start provides school enrichment, health, and nutrition services. To be eligible, a child must live in a family whose income is below the federal poverty line.

Pell Grants. This educational support program began in 1971 under the Basic Education Opportunities Grant. It is funded entirely by the federal government, which also sets eligibility requirements. Students whose family income is below a specified level qualify if they are working toward their first bachelor of arts (B.A.) degree at an accredited institution.

ENERGY ASSISTANCE

Low-income Energy Assistance. This program was established under Title 25 of the Omnibus Reconciliation Act of 1981. Eligible households receive funds for heating, cooling, weather-related, and emergency needs. States are required to do outreach and may contribute to the federal grant; they decide how to spend the block grant but must conform to the federal requirement to serve all families with income at or below 110% of the federal poverty level. Some states extend coverage to families with higher incomes.

SERVICES

Child Support Enforcement (CSE). This program was enacted in 1975 to increase the amount of child support payments collected. It handles an estimated 50% of all child support cases. The federal government reimburses each state 66% of the cost of administering its program. It also refunds a large share of the costs of establishing paternity and tracking delinquent parents.

Legal Services. The Legal Services Corporation, established in 1974, is funded by federal grants to 323 providers around the nation. It provides legal help to poor people in civil (not criminal) matters, including family law, consumer fraud, housing, jobs, education, and entitlement benefits.

JOB TRAINING

Job Opportunities and Basic Skills (JOBS) Program. The JOBS program was enacted in 1988 as part of the Family Support Act. Its purpose is to give AFDC recipients an opportunity to obtain education, training, and employment that would help them avoid long-term welfare dependency. The act extended the requirement for employment-related activity to mothers with children as young as 3 and required JOBS to offer specified educational, job skills, and placement services. The program is funded through a federal-state cost-sharing arrangement that varies from state to state; the federal share is limited to a legislated maximum.

Summer Youth Employment Program. This program is part of the 1982 Job Training and Partnership Act that provides summer employment, training, and academic services to income-eligible youths age 14 to 21. States receive funding from the federal government and have considerable leeway in its distribution. They may contribute funds for additional youth employment programs.

HOUSING

Low-Rent Public Housing. The Housing Act of 1937 was one of the earliest federal rental housing programs. Public housing projects are owned, managed, and administered by local public housing agencies. Eligibility requirements are set by the federal government on the basis of income, age, and disability. Rent charged cannot exceed 30% of monthly income.

Housing Assistance (Section 8). This program provides eligible families with rental supplements paid directly to participating owners of private-sector rental housing. Funds come from federal, state, and local governments. The assisted occupants are required to contribute up to 30% of family income toward rent.

GUIDE TO ORGANIZATIONS AND RESOURCE CENTERS

AGING

Gray Panthers
2025 Pennsylvania Avenue NW,
Suite 821
Washington, DC 20006
202-466-3132
Promotes intergenerational coordination and activism on many social issues, including national health care, affordable housing, environmental preservation, peace, ending discrimination, education, economic and tax justice, and social justice.

National Caucus and Center on Black Aged
1424 K Street NW, Suite 500
Washington, DC 20005
202-637-8400
Advocates improvements in living conditions for low-income elderly Americans, particularly blacks.

CONSUMER RIGHTS/CORPORATE RESPONSIBILITY

Public Citizen
215 Pennsylvania Avenue SE
Washington, DC 20003
202-546-4996
A nonprofit citizen research, lobbying, and litigation organization that fights for consumer rights in the marketplace, a healthy environment and workplace, clean and safe energy resources, and corporate and government accountability.

ECONOMICS (GENERAL)

Center for Popular Economics
P.O. Box 785
Amherst, MA 01004
413-545-0743
Provides economic literacy workshops for progressive organizations and individuals on a wide range of issues, including general economic literacy, international economics, urban economics, and community economic development. Also publishes books and articles.

Economic Policy Institute
1660 L Street NW
Washington, DC 20036
202-775-8810
Conducts research and promotes dialogue on economic policy issues, particularly the economics of poverty, unemployment, inflation, American industry, international competitiveness, and problems of economic adjustment as they affect people.

FAITH-BASED GROUPS WORKING ON ECONOMIC JUSTICE

American Friends Service Committee
1501 Cherry Street
Philadelphia, PA 19102
215-241-7000
Founded by the Society of Friends (Quakers), AFSC includes people of all faiths who share a vision of social justice and nonviolence.

Unitarian Universalist Service Committee

130 Prospect Street
Cambridge, MA 02139-1845
617-868-6600

Through its nonsectarian programs, the UUSC supports grassroots activism in the U.S. and overseas. It also educates and mobilizes U.S. citizens on policy issues.

FEDERAL AND LOCAL PUBLIC SPENDING

Center on Budget and Policy Priorities

777 Capital Street NE, Suite 705
Washington, DC 20002
202-408-1080

Provides research and information on federal and state government funding programs that affect low- and moderate-income people. Conducts special studies on minorities and poverty.

Common Agenda

424 C Street NE
Washington, DC 20002
202-544-8222

A coalition of national and local groups working on budget priorities.

National Priorities Project

160 Main Street, Suite 6
Northampton, MA 01060
413-584-9556

Committed to the effective involvement of citizens in directly determining the nation's priorities. Provides explanatory materials that show the impact of federal budget decisions on local communities.

HOUSING/HOMELESS

Low Income Housing Coalition

1012 Fourteenth Street NW, Suite 1200
Washington, DC 20005
202-662-1530

Educates the public and organizations about low-income housing through conferences, publications, and technical assistance.

National Coalition for the Homeless

1612 K Street NW, Suite 1004
Washington, DC 20006
202-775-1322

Provides information and education to people and organizations working with the homeless and promotes housing for low-income families.

HUNGER

Food Research and Action Center

1875 Connecticut Avenue NW, Suite 540
Washington, DC 20009
202-986-2200

Seeks to enhance public awareness of the problems of hunger and poverty and provides assistance to groups working on these issues.

IMMIGRANT AND REFUGEE RIGHTS

Center for Immigrants Rights

48 St. Marks Place, Fourth Floor
New York, NY 10003
212-505-6890

Provides information to immigrants, offers advice on immigration law, and supports efforts to reform public policy.

National Network for Immigrant and Refugee Rights

310 Eighth Street, Suite 307
Oakland, CA 94607
510-465-1984

Coordinates national campaigns and projects on immigrant and refugee rights.

INCOME DISTRIBUTION

Share the Wealth

35 Hampstead Street

Boston, MA 02130

617-423-2148

Educates people on how inequality and the maldistribution of wealth are jeopardizing the future security and prosperity of our nation.

LABOR AND WORK

9 to 5 Working Women Education Fund

614 Superior Avenue NW

Cleveland, OH 44113

414-274-0933

Conducts research on the concerns of women office workers.

Federation for Industrial Retention and Renewal

3411 West Diversey, Suite 10

Chicago, IL 60647

312-252-7676

A national network of projects promoting community-based industrial policy and economic development.

Jobs with Justice

501 Third Street

Washington, DC 20001

202-434-1106

A national campaign for workers' rights; local chapters include coalitions of religious, labor, and community organizations active throughout the country.

National Jobs for All Coalition

475 Riverside Drive, Room 853

New York, NY 10115

212-870-3064

Dedicated to providing jobs with sufficient pay for all who want them and to demonstrating the linkages between unemployment and other problems facing the nation, such as women's rights, the environment, and economic justice.

MEDIA

Fairness and Accuracy in Reporting (FAIR)

130 West Twenty-Fifth Street

New York, NY 10001

212-633-6700

A media-watch organization advocating pluralism in media. Maintains a speaker's bureau, compiles statistics, and publishes a magazine.

National Radio Project

830 Los Trancos Road

Portola Valley, CA 94208

415-851-7256

Devoted to airing popular and progressive voices in the media. Broadcasts a weekly radio show entitled *Making Contact* that focuses on current issues; available free to every public radio station in the U.S. and Canada.

ORGANIZING AND COMMUNITY ACTION

Association of Community Organizations for Reform Now (ACORN)

1024 Elysian Fields Avenue

New Orleans, LA 70117

504-943-0044

Advocates for local involvement and control over issues affecting communities.

Center for Community Change

1000 Wisconsin Avenue NW
Washington, DC 20007
202-342-0567
Helps local groups run by low-income people to organize themselves and their communities, build affordable housing, and develop successful issue campaigns.

Center for Third World Organizing

1218 East Twenty-First Street
Oakland, CA 94604
510-533-7583
National organization dedicated to the struggle for social and economic justice for low-income people and people of color.

National Rainbow Coalition

1700 K Street NW, Suite 800
Washington, DC 20006
202-728-1180
Encourages the development of a progressive political leadership dedicated to economic justice, peace, and human rights.

PEOPLE OF COLOR

Joint Center for Political and Economic Studies

1301 Pennsylvania Avenue NW,
Suite 400
Washington, DC 20004
202-789-3500
Through research and information dissemination, aims to improve the socioeconomic status of black Americans, increase their influence in the political and public policy arenas, and facilitate the building of coalitions across race lines.

National Association for the Advancement of Colored People (NAACP)

4805 Mount Hope Drive
Baltimore, MD 21215
410-358-8900
Works to achieve equal rights through the democratic process and to eliminate racial prejudice by removing discrimination in housing, employment, voting, education, the courts, transportation, recreation, and business.

National Council of La Raza

1111 Nineteenth Street NW,
Suite 1000
Washington, DC 20036
202-310-9000
National umbrella organization working for civil rights and economic opportunities for Latinos.

National Urban League

500 East Sixty-Second Street
New York, NY 10021
212-310-9000
Works for racial equality for African-Americans and other minorities in all phases of life. Fights institutional racism and provides direct service to minorities in the areas of employment, housing, education, social welfare, health, law, consumer rights, and community and minority business development.

POVERTY AND WELFARE POLICY

Center for Law and Social Policy (CLASP)

1616 P Street NW, Suite 150
Washington, DC 20036
202-328-5140
Conducts research and policy analysis on issues affecting low-income families.

Center on Social Welfare Policy and Law

275 Seventh Avenue, Sixth Floor
New York, NY 10001
212-633-6967
A national legal and policy organization that focuses on means-tested cash public assistance programs. Provides representation for poor people in litigation and before administrative and legislative bodies and analysis of developments in welfare law, training, and individualized assistance for local welfare advocates.

Coalition on Human Needs

1000 Wisconsin Avenue NW
Washington, DC 20007
202-342-0726
An alliance of over 100 national organizations working together to promote public policies that address the needs of low-income and other vulnerable Americans. Promotes adequate funding for human needs programs, progressive tax policies, and other federal measures and serves as an information clearinghouse.

Institute for Research on Poverty

1180 Observatory Drive
3412 Social Science Building
University of Wisconsin–Madison
Madison, WI 53706
608-262-6358
Organizes conferences and publishes papers on all aspects of poverty.

REPRODUCTIVE RIGHTS

Planned Parenthood Federation of America

810 Seventh Avenue
New York, NY 10019
212-541-7800
Provides leadership in making effective means of voluntary fertility regulation (including contraception, abortion, sterilization, and infertility services) available and fully accessible to all.

WOMEN

Institute for Women's Policy Research

1400 Twentieth Street NW,
Suite 104
Washington, DC 20036
202-785-5100
Researches economic issues important to women and families, including low-wage work, poverty, welfare reform, child care, family leave, contingent work, pay equity, and health care.

National Organization of Women

1000 Sixteenth Street NW
Suite 700
Washington, DC 20036
202-331-0066
Works to end discrimination and gender inequality in all facets of life and to increase the number of women elected to political office. Open to all who support gender equality.

Wider Opportunities for Women

815 Fifteenth Street NW
Suite 916
Washington, DC 20005
202-638-3143
Works nationally and locally to achieve economic independence and equality of opportunity for women and girls. Provides organizing, skills training, and technical assistance for women workers.

YOUTH AND FAMILIES

Child Care Law Center

22 Second Street, Fifth Floor
San Francisco, CA 94105
415-495-5498
Monitors legislation that relates to child care issues. Provides training, technical assistance, and legal services to advocates working on behalf of child care for low-income families.

Children's Defense Fund

25 E Street NW
Washington, DC 20001
202-628-8787
Provides research, advocacy, public education, written materials, monitoring of federal agencies, assistance to state and local groups, and community organizing on a wide range of issues that affect children and youth.

GUIDE TO RESEARCH MATERIALS

Statistical Abstract of the United States. The best source of general economic data. Published annually by the U.S. Bureau of the Census. Available from the Government Printing Office (GPO), Superintendent of Documents, Stop SM, Washington, DC 20402. To order materials from the GPO call 202-512-1800 or fax to 202-512-2250.

Green Book, or Background Material and Data on Major Programs within the Jurisdiction of the Committee on Ways and Means (of the U.S. House of Representatives). The best source of detailed information on major federal entitlement programs. Available from the GPO.

Income, Poverty, and Valuation of Noncash Benefits, Current Population Reports (CPR), Series P-60. In March of every year, the Bureau of the Census conducts an extensive survey of 1 out of every 1,000 U.S. families to determine trends in income and poverty. The results are published annually in their *Current Population Reports.* Available from the GPO.

Dollars and Sense. A bimonthly magazine containing short and interesting articles about current economic events. Published by the Economic Affairs Bureau, Inc., 1 Summer Street, Somerville, MA 02143, 617-628-8411.

Focus. A quarterly publication of the Institute for Research on Poverty. Free. Can be requested directly from the institute. See page 142 for contact information.

The Grassroots Economic Organizing Newsletter. An excellent resource for networking with grassroots groups and researching funding opportunities. Published six times a year. Contact GEO, P.O. Box 5065, New Haven CT 06525, 203-389-6194.

Insight & Action: The Human Needs Report. A bimonthly newsletter and legislative update published by the Coalition on Human Needs.

See page 142 for contact information.

Poverty & Race. Contains topical articles as well as listings of recent reports and meetings. Published six times a year by the Poverty & Race Research Action Council, 1711 Connecticut Avenue NW, Room 207, Washington, DC 20009, 202-387-9887.

Update. Lists the most recent developments in welfare issues. Published by the Center for Law and Social Policy. Number of issues per year varies. Subscriptions also include the quarterly newsletter, *Family Matters.* See page 142 for contact information.

Welfare News. Tracks recent legislative developments. Published by the Center on Social Welfare Policy and Law. See page 142 for contact information.

BG	*Boston Globe* (daily)
BLS	Bureau of Labor Statistics
CPE	Center for Popular Economics
CPR	Bureau of the Census, Current Population Reports (Washington, DC: Government Printing Office, various years).
CSM	*Christian Science Monitor* (daily)
GAO	General Accounting Office
GPO	Government Printing Office
IWPR	Institute for Women's Policy Research
LAT	*Los Angeles Times* (daily)
NYT	*New York Times* (daily)
SA	*Statistical Abstract of the U.S.* (Washington, DC: Government Printing Office, various years).
USNWR	*U.S. News and World Report* (weekly)
WP	*Washington Post* (daily)
WSJ	*Wall Street Journal* (daily)
1994 Green Book	Committee on Ways and Means, U.S./House of Representatives, *Overview of Entitlement Programs, 1994 Green Book* (Washington, DC: Government Printing Office, 1994).

The information in this section comes from a variety of sources, including "Welfare Reform," *Congressional Digest* (June–July 1995): 166–167; General Accounting Office Report to the Chairman, Subcommittee on Children, Family, Drugs, and Alcoholism, Committee on Labor and Human Resources, U.S. Senate, *Infants and Toddlers: Dramatic Increases in Numbers Living in Poverty* (Washington, DC, Apr. 1994); "Social Security Programs in the United States," *Social Security Bulletin* 52 (July 1989): 2–78; Office of U.S. Representative John Olver (D–Massachusetts); *The Budget of the United States, FY1996* (Washington, DC: GPO, 1995); and Center for Budget and Policy Priorities, *States and the Poor: How Budget Decisions Affect Low-Income Families* (Washington, DC, February 1993).

Some information in this section is based on Carolyn A. Fisher and Carol A. Schwartz, eds. *Encyclopedia of Associations 1996*, 30th ed. (New York: Gale Research Inc., 1995).